SAMUEL JOHNSON'S EARLY BIOGRAPHERS

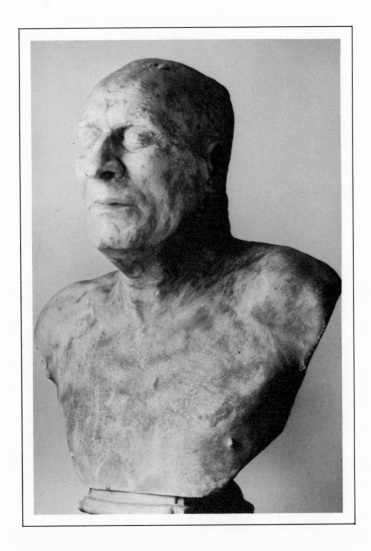

SAMUEL JOHNSON'S
EARLY
BIOGRAPHERS

ROBERT E. KELLEY

AND

O M BRACK, JR.

Ψ

UNIVERSITY OF IOWA PRESS

IOWA CITY

Library of Congress Catalog Card Number: 74-151649
University of Iowa Press, Iowa City, Iowa 52240

ISBN 87745-021-8

CONTENTS

ILLUSTRATIONS

PREFACE

Long before his death on 13 December 1784, Samuel Johnson was public property. Almost immediately after Johnson died one of his earliest biographers, Thomas Tyers, proclaimed: "He belonged to the world at large." Johnson's final illness and death were, to say the least, national events. An obituary notice in the *Gentleman's Magazine* for December 1784, which followed a eulogy by "Albanicus," a Scot, referred to the "remarkably affectionate suspense of the publick" during Johnson's final months. William Gerard Hamilton, Johnson's close friend, expressed the general sentiment in moving terms: "He has made a chasm, which not only nothing can fill up, but which nothing has a tendency to fill up. Johnson is dead. Let us go to the next best. There is nobody; no man can be said to put you in mind of Johnson." Both Arthur Murphy and Hannah More mentioned the great effect that Johnson's passing had on the literary world. Dr. Michael Lort wrote Bishop Percy in May 1785, that Johnson's death afforded a "fruitful" topic of conversation for three weeks. Almost two years later, in a letter to Percy, Boswell indicated, with some qualification, that the light of Johnson's memory had not dimmed:

> Though the magnitude and lustre of his character make Doctor Johnson an object of the public attention longer than almost any person whom we have known, yet there is some danger that if the publication of his life be delayed too long, curiosity may be fainter.[1]

Much of this interest was heightened, of course, by Johnson's well-known fear of Judgment combined with his courage in the face of death. Apart from the usual ghoulish interest in the passing of great public figures, the avid concern of Johnson's contemporaries was no doubt motivated by the didactic importance of a Christian death, especially that of a moralist such as Johnson. His death was often treated as an illustration of religious and ethical instruction.

With all this manifest curiosity regarding Johnson's death, it is little wonder that widespread interest should arise about his life. That Johnson dead was of almost as much service to the booksellers as Johnson alive was attested to by the fund of material which appeared between his death and the publication, on 16 May 1791, of James Boswell's monumental *Life of Samuel Johnson, LL.D.* Newspapers and periodicals printed Johnsoniana with astonishing frequency in an attempt to satisfy the voracious appetites of their readers with collections of Johnson's *bon mots,* "table-talk," with scraps of his sermons, with letters to, by, and about him, with anecdotes by his friends and enemies, with character sketches, with copies of his will, with accounts of his last days, and with elegies, eulogies, and epitaphs. Even before his death Johnson had been the subject of several sketches and biographies. Of more importance, however, are the materials published between the "Memoirs of the Life and Writings of Dr. Samuel Johnson" which appeared in the *Universal Magazine* for August 1784 and the appearance of Boswell's biography. Between 1784 and 1791, at least eleven formal or semi-formal biographies of Johnson were published. In addition to the better-known writings of Boswell, Mrs. Piozzi, and Hawkins, there were biographies written by Thomas Tyers, William Cooke, William Shaw, Joseph Towers, and several anonymous writers. It is with these lesser-known productions that this study is concerned.

Biographies or lives, for the purposes of this study,

are those writings which attempt to deal with John-son's life, including his birth and early years, in some way, however slight. We have ignored the three major contemporary biographies of Johnson, except when they bear directly on these lesser lives, because they have received extended treatment elsewhere. We have excluded those lives published before 1784 on the grounds that they are, for the most part, mere recitals of facts which eventually found their way into later biographies, and that they offer no meaningful atti-tudes about Johnson (see Appendix B). Some attention is given to the context in which these early lives of Johnson appeared because the prevailing critical opin-ions, such as they were, greatly influenced these biog-raphies, and an awareness of contemporary opinions of biography's purpose and methods is necessary if we are to understand the early lives fully. There can be little doubt that some of these lives provoked valuable comment on the nature of biography, and forced some critics to consider more closely than before the precise aims and techniques of biography. More important for Johnson scholars, these early lives place the major biographies in historical perspective.

Johnson, of course, meant various things to various people. It would be surprising indeed if the early bi-ographies expressed uniform opinions of him. It can be shown, however, that the approach to Johnson taken by each biographer was more or less dependent on the depth of his acquaintance — or lack thereof — with

Johnson. But these lives, taken together, convey two dominant images of Johnson: as writer and as moralist.

This is not to say, of course, that the biographers were themselves aware that their works fell into such a scheme, nor do we wish to fit them into an artificially constructed pattern. In most cases, the pre-eminent concern with, say, Johnson the moralist was re-enforced by reference to his writings. Nevertheless, this grouping of the biographies seems to be valid because it gives us an insight into the contemporary presentation and evaluation of Johnson's life and career.

This extended essay on the early lives of Samuel Johnson has grown out of our original and much larger project of preparing an annotated edition of these lives. For several reasons, there has been little attempt to trace the numerous biographical anecdotes about Johnson which appeared in the newspapers. In the first place, collecting all of the anecdotes from the newspapers would be a mindless and expensive job that would take years to complete. Even then, the authenticity of most of the anecdotes would be impossible to establish. Finding that a particular anecdote used by one of the biographers had appeared earlier in print is no guarantee that this was his source. As our essay reveals, the biographers borrowed heavily from one another and drew, no doubt, on a body of biographical information which must have had a history of oral transmission. When new materials were introduced, the most likely explanation is that the information came from Johnson or one of his friends, since most of the biographers had some connection, however slight, with Johnson and his circle.

We are grateful for the assistance we have received in preparing this study. Portions of the manuscript, in earlier drafts, were read by W. R. Irwin, James L. Clifford, Philip B. Daghlian, Malvin R. Zirker, and Philip R. Wikelund. For assistance of various kinds we are indebted to John V. Price, Lois Fields, Sharon Graves, Vince Heinrichs, Mary Jane Jones, Donald Stefanson, and Robert and Catherine Ward. We thank the staff of the Beinecke Rare Book and Manuscript Library, especially Kenneth Nesheim, for patience and good humor in answering our inquiries. In particular we wish to acknowledge the invaluable assistance of Herman W. Liebert. With characteristic generosity, he has given freely of his time and advice and has kindly made available to us the resources of his own library. To our wives, Judy Kelley and Vida Brack, we are grateful for patience and encouragement.

R. E. K.
O M B., Jr.

CHAPTER ONE

RIVALRIES

Throughout the eighteenth century there were two conflicting attitudes towards biography — that it should present its subject in general terms as an impeccable hero and that it should present its subject as a human being whose personal foibles were not to be ignored.[1] Both notions, however, were influenced by the nature of the audience which biography commanded. The steady growth of the reading public was matched by its corresponding influence on the type of biography written in the period. Some biographers and most critics upheld the idea that as an instructive medium biography had to be discreet. The more eminent the subject, the more harm done by thoughtless biography and the greater the care needed to render his life in fitting moral terms. But what of the general reading public? A large portion of the public, in opposition to the critics, was not interested in reading lectures on the human embodiment of virtue; rather, they sought to be entertained, to admire the subject on grounds not exclusively moral. Consequently, much biography was intended to gratify the taste of these readers, and colorful if concocted lives of criminals, soldiers, explorers, and members of high society were published to satisfy the thirst for exciting incident, personality, and spectacle. Often, moral concerns were obscured or ignored.

The gratification of this kind of biographical interest was accomplished largely through the publication of pamphlets, catch-penny guides, character sketches, letters, journals, death-bed confessions, biographical dictionaries and prefaces to collected works, and reviews in newspapers and periodicals. The popularity of these outlets for indiscreet biography revealed a vigorous public interest, even though it diverted biography from its main channel into tributary streams. The proponents of discreet biography eventually had to face the fact that literary gossip had become almost a way of life, and that newspaper and magazine chroniclers had become increasingly less inclined to suppress data, no matter how trivial or compromising.

In light of this situation, it is no wonder that the early lives of Johnson were frequently held up to scorn by reviewers, chiefly because they refused to believe that nonentities could write biography with dignity and honesty. Most of the vituperation was directed against the three best-known biographers: Boswell, Hawkins, and Mrs. Piozzi. The others merited surprisingly little consideration, although often condemned collectively. Almost as soon as all of these biographies were published, the ridicule of the biographers became a national pastime.[2]

Much of this material, to be sure, was decidedly trivial, but it revealed the extreme reactions which Johnsoniana inspired. Front-page coverage was given, for example, to the progress of the subscriptions for Johnson's monument in Westminster Abbey, to the specious discovery of a lost epigram by Johnson, and to Johnson's favorite willow tree near Lichfield (complete with illustration of the candidate).[3] At any rate, the dominant tone of the observations on the early biographies was one of horror and dismay that the reputation of so sturdy a moral example should be tainted and betrayed, especially by Johnson's "friends." [4] Typical of the almost interminable epigrammatic assaults on Johnson's biographer-friends was that of the *Morning Post* of 23 April 1791:

> Dr. Johnson's fate resembles that of the *Great Ox.* — They were both gigantic . . . both shown by their *friends* for a time, and both, after being knocked on the head, have *cut up well!*

Even more to the point was the following comment in the *London Packet* of 29–31 December 1784:

> So many scribblers are at work to finish Dr. Johnson's life, that it is a wonder that his death was not more *sudden*. The absurd nonsense which the *half-witted* and crazy friends of Dr. Johnson have published, has done more to injure his memory than the worst failing that ever could be imputed to him.[5]

Two men, Dr. Samuel Parr and Dr. Charles Burney, expressed privately their distress over the early biographies. Parr, who was not so intimate with Johnson as Burney, remarked: "Now that the old lion is dead, every ass thinks he may kick at him." [6] To rectify this situation, Parr considered writing a biography of Johnson, a life which would have contained a full review of European literature and, claimed its would-be author, would have been the "third most learned work that has ever appeared." [7] Comparing his projected volume to Boswell's he remarked that it "should have been, not the droppings of his lips, but the history of his mind." [8] Despite his ambitious aim to write both a "Life and Times" biography and a psychological study, Parr abandoned his project in 1812; his sole contribution to Johnson biography was his Latin inscription for Johnson's monument.[9]

A VIEW NEAR LICHFIELD, INCLUDING JOHNSON'S FAVORITE WILLOW TREE

Burney, who candidly revealed his deep admiration for Johnson in a letter to Thomas Twining written in October 1781, was incensed at what he judged the callousness of the early lives. Writing to Twining five days after Johnson's funeral, he expressed his fears of the "six or eight" biographers who had already announced their intentions.[10] Like some other members of the Streatham circle, Burney took notes on Johnson, and no doubt seriously contemplated a biography of his close friend. He was aroused partly by the knowledge that his enemy, Hawkins, with whom he had feuded when both were writing their histories of music, was also preparing a life of Johnson.[11] Much of the bitterness against other biographies in the following passage can be explained by his antipathy to Hawkins:

> I will only tell you [Susan Phillips] the Names of these last who are already writing his Life: Sir John *Hawkins,* one of his Executors with Dr Scott . . . & Sir Jos. Reynolds — Dr Kippis: *Croft* whose life of the poet Dr Young is inserted in Johnson's Lives: *Boswell;* Tommy Tyers; The Editor of the Johnsoniana, a Mr Cook, who does not set his name to it, but who suffered Kearsley to advertise it as ready for publication the day after the good soul's death, & it is to be published tomorrow. Be-

sides these a life of him is publishing every day in one of the News papers. Not one of these Biographers has to my thinking a single Qualification necessary for the work he so flippantly undertakes; nor one who sufficiently reverenced his learning, Genius, & Piety; or who is possessed of a style & abilities capable of doing them any justice. Hawkins & Kippis are both equally dry & dull — Croft, a fop who imitates Johnson's style without being possessed of one of his Ideas . . . . Tommy Tyers is such a quaint, feeble, fumble-fisted writer, as is only fit for Mother Goose's tales — & Boswell with all his Anecdotes, will only make a story book, a kind of Joe Miller the 2^d without address or dignity of introduction or application in relating his bon mots — and Cook, if we may judge of his talents by the Johnsoniana, will continue to spoil the best stories he picked up, by want of powers to relate them.[12]

Obviously, Burney's anger obscured his usually clear judgment, particularly with reference to Boswell and Tyers. Kippis and Croft apparently abandoned their projects. So, for that matter, did Burney. According to an obituary notice he gave up his intentions because "the subject was so overwhelmed by various publications." [13] That he did so, for whatever reason, is regrettable, for he knew Johnson well, and possessed the intelligence and sensitivity necessary to the production of biography.

These biographies elicited both vituperative and favorable reviews and letters to the editor, and the newspapers and periodicals were filled with countless manifestations of alarm — some serious, some not — over the forwardness of Johnson's biographers.[14] By and large, the late eighteenth-century press, with few exceptions, displayed little concern for responsible criticism. Abuse and witty display was commonplace and often passed for literary criticism.[15] Under such license, almost any form of reaction to the biographies, no matter how careless or gross, found its way into print with little difficulty. And the proliferation of such material, with its hyperbolic execrations, increased the sale of the very books it was designed to chastise. Boswell, for one, was never averse to making the most of a bad press. In a sense, those who attacked the biographers as mere opportunists were little better themselves, and the irresponsibility of much of their criticism was at once a result of and an index to their opportunism. A further measure of this irresponsibility was the inevitable overflow of satire heaped on Johnson — if the so-called critics blamed his biographers for revealing his weaknesses, they also berated Johnson for giving "scandalmongers" the chance to do so. Quite often Johnson and his biographers were condemned in the same breath. Critics derided the biographers for trying to apotheosize a man, who, because of his prejudices, religious fear, and political beliefs, scarcely deserved apotheosis, or for revealing his faults to public view, in which case the biographers were charged with betrayal of friendship and duty. The following is a representative attack:

> Such is the portrait his friends have delineated; and whatever they suffered from the brutality of the living, has been amply revenged on the memory of the dead. Instead of the amiable philosopher diffusing satisfaction to all who approached him, they tell us of an imperious pedant, cruel in his mirth, and fierce in his resentment. Instead of a friend to liberty, they unmasked the abetter of arbitrary powers. For piety, they give us superstition; for judgment, dogmatical incredulity.[16]

The irony of this outburst and countless others like it was that the newspapers and magazines themselves began to publish their own anecdotes of Johnson soon after he died (borrowing most of them from the biographies), thereby contributing to the proliferation of Johnsoniana which they deplored.

More often than not, the papers and magazines responded to this material by printing biting doggerel against the biographers. However pungent or comic, these poems betrayed an undercurrent of shock and dismay at the alleged mistreatment of Johnson. One of the most vocal detractors was George Colman the Elder, whose epigram appeared in the *St. James's Chronicle* for 12–14 June 1787:

> Thee, Johnson, both dead and alive we may note
>   In the fam'd Biographical Line,
> When living the Life of a SAVAGE you wrote,
>   Now many a Savage writes thine.[17]

Soame Jenyns expressed his feelings in more graphic terms:

> Here lies poor Johnson. Reader, have a care,
> Tread lightly, lest you rouse a sleeping bear;
> Religious — moral — gen'rous and humane
> He was — but self-sufficient, rude and vain:
> Ill-bred and over-bearing in dispute
> A scholar and a Christian — yet a brute.
> Would you know all his wisdom and his folly,
> His actions — sayings — mirth and melancholy,
> BOSWELL AND THRALE, retailers of his wit,
> Will tell you how he wrote, and talk'd, and
>   cough'd and spit.[18]

At other times, the complaints registered in the press were less virulent and more sympathetic towards Johnson. The *Morning Post,* to illustrate, lamented on 12 March 1788, that "Poor Dr. JOHNSON has been served up to us in every shape — We have had him boiled to a rag, *roasted, fricassed,* and now we are to have him scraped into a sermon on his wife's death." Scarcely two weeks later, aware that Boswell's *Life,* a volume of "no small corpulency," was in progress, the same organ cried: "Formerly when the brains were out, the man were dead, but poor Dr. JOHNSON, *with more lives than a cat,* revives only to be killed again." Again, we may note the popularity of the notion that the biographers, especially those intimate with Johnson, were murderers of his reputation. The analogy had its point, for the indignation aroused against the biographies and Johnsoniana was coupled with the realization that the dead Johnson could not defend himself. The implication, of course, was that such publications would never have been written had Johnson been alive. To the charge of murder, therefore, was added the more odious accusation of cowardice. But this argument was groundless, for Johnson seldom replied to his detractors and it was unlikely that he would have spoken out against these biographers.

Apart from the works of Boswell, Hawkins, and Mrs. Piozzi only one other early biography, Cooke's *Life,* met with widespread censure. Most of the criticism — that it was riddled with factual and interpretative errors, with trifling anecdotes, with imprecise character delineation, all written in a pedestrian style — pointed towards the haste with which this work was composed.[19] As the reviewer in the *Town and Country Magazine* put it, Cooke's was a "hasty publication, put together for the benefit of the bookseller and author, with all possible expedition . . . . If being foremost in the field constitutes any merit, this literary jockey will win the plate." [20] These charges of haste were, to some degree, well-founded. The volume was advertised, according to the *Gentleman's Magazine*, "before the Doctor had been two days dead, and was published on the ninth morning" after Johnson's passing.[21] Kearsley's announcement in the *St. James's Chronicle* for 18–21 December was an effort to forestall criticism by begging the public to withhold judgment until after the book's appearance and by setting forth Cooke's qualifications as Johnson's biographer, qualifications which were in some measure exaggerated.[22] In addition, Kearsley's announcement tried to avoid charges of haste by swearing that the book had been long finished, but withheld from publication out of delicacy. Kearsley's position was, of course, at least partially weakened when the reviewers pointed out precise examples of haste in the *Life*. Thus the alternatives to the problem were that the book was either written and published in extreme haste, or was already in press before Johnson actually died. The latter seems more likely.[23] That Cooke's talent (if he was blessed with any) did not lie within the province of revision can be attested by the unsatisfactory reviews of the second edition of the *Life* (1785) in which many errors

remained uncorrected.[24] The reviews of Cooke's biography were, for the most part, accurate and fair,
much fairer than those of Boswell, Hawkins, and Mrs.
Piozzi.

But not all of the responses to the early lives were
hostile. For example, in a letter to the *Gentleman's
Magazine* over the signature "S.J." a lady praised the
Johnsoniana which had appeared because it aided the
cause of virtue and presented faithful pictures of
Johnson's mind and heart. In the same issue, one
"E.R.R." observed that a supplemental life of Johnson
was needed in order to synthesize the Johnsoniana already in print.[25] William Hayley included in the first
dialogue of his *Two Dialogues, Containing a Compar-
ative View of the Lives, Characters, and Writings, of
Philip, Late Earl of Chesterfield, and Dr. Samuel Johnson* (1787), a brief discussion between the Archdeacon
and the Colonel regarding the merits of the earlier
lives.[26] The Colonel described the biographers as
"busy children" and Johnson's "little flock" who,
seeking to transform Johnson from a shilling to a
guinea, had merely revealed the base metal of which
he was made. Ultimately, he argued, the biographers
were instruments of poetic justice giving Johnson his
due by revealing his weaknesses for all to see. To this
charge the Archdeacon replied that the biographers
were an "honest, philosophical set of people" whose
veneration for Johnson led not to partiality but to a
series of balanced estimates. The Archdeacon further
characterized the attacks on Johnson's biographers as

examples of the "pride of ignorance" and the "malice of envy."

The Archdeacon's opinion seems to have been a fairly accurate index to the contemporary response to Towers's biography. When Bishop Lort wrote to Thomas Percy on 16 December 1786, that Towers's *Essay* contributed nothing new to the knowledge of Johnson's life, but that it was fair to its subject in all but political matters, he voiced the general opinion of the work.[27] The commentator in the *English Review* noted the lack of originality but thought that the chief object of the author was to attack Johnson's political principles which, he agreed, were open to objection. On the whole the pamphlet was praised as candid and impartial and highly favorable to the character of Johnson.[28] The *Monthly Review* also acknowledged its lack of originality, but commended its critical balance, honesty, and justice.[29] Rather surprising, in view of the *Monthly*'s general practice of attacking those biographies which censured Johnson, was the omission of any reference to Towers's diatribe against Johnson's political views and his treatment of Milton. On the other hand, the writer for the *Critical Review* was careful to point out Towers's unthinking views on Johnson's political tracts while at the same time praising Towers's evaluation of Johnson's non-political writings.[30] The reviewer admitted, however, that as biography it was both incomplete and hackneyed, faults which he felt were overcome by Towers's critical perspicacity.

From the foregoing comments, it is evident that some of the early biographies of Johnson merited little individual attention.[31] It was, after all, much easier to attempt to destroy them as a group than to discuss them individually, in which case their good points and valuable insights stood a better chance of being disclosed. Furthermore, because none of these biographers was well known in literary circles it might have been considered a waste of space to devote much critical attention to their works except as a group.[32] Nevertheless, when discussed individually in separate reviews, these lives won greater approval than might have been expected in view of the widespread condemnation of Johnsoniana.

The contemporary critical reactions to the early biographies revealed quite clearly that the belief in the biographer as a sort of traitor was still alive despite the inroads made on the theory of biographical primness by such critics as Johnson himself. The modes of biographical treachery — to the subject and to the genre — are, of course, legion: unwarranted suppression or invention, the temptation to sit in judgment, slight juggling of dates, the placing of a crucial document or record of conversation at its most effective spot. It is, in other words, almost impossible for any biographer to complete his task with a total absence of emotional, intellectual, moral, critical, or political prejudices for or against his subject. All of these forms of bias exist in one or another of the early biographers of Johnson, but, as in the case of Tyers, it is obvious that such prejudices, once recognized, may lend a definite charm and color to the account without necessarily detracting from its merits. With Towers, bias worked to the opposite effect. The answer to such prejudices in biography is not, as some critics would have it, the donning of blinders to everything about a man's life except verifiable fact. The biographer cannot be impartial, nor would he wish to be. Similarly, the intrusions of Mrs. Piozzi and Boswell into their own portraits of Johnson, often censured by nineteenth-century critics, we now find appealing, if a little overplayed. The dictum that the biographer, like a child, should be neither seen nor heard is hardly practicable or desirable when the biographer happens to be the friend of his subject. In this respect, Shaw's intrusion into his account, although somewhat jarring in context and vain in tone, provided valuable background concerning Johnson's part in the Ossian controversy. Furthermore, those who reproach the biographer for intruding his presence where it is not wanted often forget that his presence may be required in order to make clear the authority for the anecdotes he relates or the judgments he renders. Frequently, the sense of the actual occurrence of a story is heightened by the biographer's bearing witness to its unfolding.

At any rate, critical and familial fear of the ever-growing intrusions of biography upon the subject's privacy, a fear most frantically expressed in the critical outbursts which followed the publication of Johnson's lives, has not abated to this day, nor has the desire, however well or maliciously intended, to capitalize on the passing of famous figures. Horatio Nelson, for example, was killed at Trafalgar on 21 October 1805. By the close of the year, seven hastily concocted biographies were published, beating any record Johnson's biographers possibly could have claimed. In the next five years, seventeen more lives of Nelson were written, only a few of them valuable.[33] Within a month of Dickens's death, three biographies appeared, all supplied by publishers who catered to public curiosity. Eminent biographers such as Boswell and Lockhart were inspired to greater efforts partly by their awareness that other contestants occupied the field; certainly this awareness, in part, prompted Boswell and Mrs. Piozzi to publish their works when they did.

The early lives of Johnson were not the only biographies to meet with stern resistance from the adherents of discretion. Carlyle's life of Froude, to name just one example, was criticized in terms which echoed the reviews of the early biographies of Johnson. But like many of these biographers, Carlyle was intent upon showing his subject as he was, not as he might — or should — have been. In our own day biographies of such widely different men as Humphrey Bogart, Ernest Hemingway, John Kennedy, and Winston Churchill have been censured on moral as well as critical grounds.

The problem in writing the life of a man like Johnson was voiced by a man who never knew him, but who faced a problem not unlike that confronted by Johnson's biographers. Joseph Spence, who has been described as Pope's Boswell, aptly pictured the difficulty of presenting Pope's mixed character in terms which suit Johnson as well:

> All the people well acquainted with Mr. Pope, looked on him as a most friendly, open, charitable, and generous-hearted man; — all the world almost, that did not know him, were got into a mode of having very different ideas of him: how proper this makes it to publish these Anecdotes after my death.[34]

Johnson's biography of Pope, with its reasonably balanced portrait, had captured much of the complex character of the man, but a less-skilled biographer conditioned to expect unwavering greatness from his hero and who preferred to ignore those events and character traits which cast shadows on the light of his heroic stature would not be alive to these subtleties.

CHAPTER TWO

JOHNSON THE WRITER

Although admired in his own time as lexicographer, biographer, critic, and poet, Johnson was never so popular a writer as Scott and Dickens were to be in the next century. Nevertheless, that several early biographers focused on Johnson as writer showed that at least part of his contemporary fame rested on his literary productions, no matter how unspectacular their success might have been. None of these early lives, however, was a critical biography, at least as we use the term today. These biographers offered little criticism of Johnson's works, nor did they explore in depth the relationship between Johnson's character and his writings. This is not to say that they effected an outright divorce between Johnson the man and Johnson the writer, but that they made no sustained attempt to use biography to help explain the art or to employ evidence in the writings to illuminate Johnson's character.

There were several reasons for this focus on Johnson the writer. Little was known of Johnson's life apart from his literary career, and most of these biographers had practically no access to whatever information was available. Another reason was the haste with which some of these biographies were written, a haste which precluded detailed investigation and exposition of his literary career, let alone his life. The most likely explanation, however, was that some biographers saw Johnson chiefly through his works and desired to project their image of Johnson by concentrating on his literary efforts rather than upon his life, though they occasionally referred to the life when they saw fit. As a result of this narrow vision, the first two lives that are discussed were biographies in title only.

I

The first life of any length or real importance focused on Johnson the writer. This was the *Memoirs of the Life and Writings of Dr. Samuel Johnson*, a nine-page article, signed by "L," which appeared in the *Universal Magazine* four months before Johnson's death and was reprinted numerous times without acknowledgment.[1]

In general, this brief essay was no better than most of the cursory journalistic biographies of the period. Although reasonably well-written, its focus was blurred by incoherent transitions between Johnson's life and his literary career, and it added little information about Johnson's life to that already known. It was valuable, however, for its contributions to the Johnson canon, and for the rather elaborate critical treatment of biography which occupied almost one-third of the article.

The opening section of the *Memoirs* dealt with the virtues, weaknesses, and appeal of biography. "L" looked upon biography as a moral instrument; however, he based his interpretation of biographical utility less on a strictly moral or ethical foundation than on the "emulation" of genius and learning that biography fostered. He concentrated on Johnson not as a moral giant but as a purely literary hero who proved that the "honours of Victory, and triumph . . . of conspicuous worth" could, with "laborious Application," be reached by any man (p. 89).

Although he recognized the moral value of biography, "L" was unwilling to conform to the rules of decorum. He made the usual distinction between biography and history, but did so in order to justify the invasion of the subject's privacy. In supporting the use of minutiae in biography, "L" cited *Rambler* No. 60, chiefly to vindicate his undertaking this biography while Johnson was still alive. The "obscure and intricate recesses of domestic life," he claimed, were the valid province of the biographer, and without this freedom, biography was neither instructive nor entertaining. Obviously then, he was convinced that trivia and private information were valuable in delineating a man's personality. He recognized, too, the mortality of factual information necessary for good biography; therefore, he ridiculed the delicacy and obstinate "uncommunicativeness" of those who, out of respect for his privacy, refused to divulge details of the subject's life (p. 90). These squeamish individuals, maintained "L," injured two parties: mankind, which was deprived of "most excellent lessons," and the subject himself, who was entitled to "every kind of posthumous distinction" (p. 90). "L" closed this introductory section with a plea for future liberality regarding the dissemination of particulars and the hope that the "attention and candour in the following Memoirs will sufficiently compensate for the want of abundance and variety" (p. 91).

The author was whistling in the wind with his prelude, for he actually touched upon no delicate or compromising incidents in Johnson's life. True, he was the first biographer to take note of Johnson's weaknesses and indiscretions, but he did not elaborate on them to the point of daring or offensiveness. With ill-disguised regret, "L" admitted that Johnson's character was unfortunately tainted by superstition, which led him to the unwise belief in the "exploded doctrine of the reality of apparitions" (p. 96). He then launched into an unflattering discussion of the Cock-Lane ghost story which had provided the enterprising Charles Churchill with the opportunity to satirize Johnson in *The Ghost*. But the long preamble was vitiated partly because the biography itself did not deal with the issues raised therein, and partly because it appeared to serve mainly as an excuse for the brevity of his presentation. Like some of the other early biographers, "L" was a better theoretician than a biographer.

His account of Johnson's early years was like almost all the others — sparse, general, and uninformative. "L" lamented the lack of information as he passed over Johnson's youth with only a surmise as to its likely features (he imprecisely gave Johnson's birth date as "about the year 1710") (p. [91]). He briefly summarized Johnson's Oxford days, his early relationships with Garrick and Hawkesworth (chiefly to show Johnson's influence on them), and his teaching career. Here the lack of material illustrated one of the prime dangers of biography — the temptation to reconstruct a man's youth from his character and the nature of his adult achievements. In this case, it led "L" to make extravagant claims for Johnson's moral and intellectual precocity based on the demonstrated intellectual and moral prowess of his later years.

Despite his implied promise of displaying Johnson as a man, "L" betrayed his hero-worship in a brief generalization upon Johnson's early life. The spectre of Johnson's possible confinement to the obscurity of a country school haunted him, as it did other biographers. "L's" aversion for this possibility led him to boast confidently that Johnson's native genius would not have been curbed by the frustrations of teaching and the dullness of country life:

> His high descent, his kindred to the Muses, could not have been concealed; and if he had not been destined to figure as the great Dictator in the Republic of Letters, he must yet have been the gentle Apollo in exile, who sung the felicity of rural life, and taught the shepherds the love of knowledge and virtue, of industry and good order (p. 92).

The element of fate in Johnson's literary career was a favorite preoccupation of several early biographers as they attempted to account for Johnson's heroic rise to literary dictatorship. It was, ultimately, a subtle if needless method of apotheosizing Johnson.

Following the brief description of Johnson's pre-London days, "L" devoted the remainder of the *Memoirs* to a survey of Johnson's works.[2] Although given primarily to an examination of Johnson as a writer, this biography contained little criticism of the works cited. Aware of his spatial limitations, "L" apologized for this omission, offering instead the conventional hope that extensive quotations, especially from *The Vanity of Human Wishes,* precluded the necessity for critical observation (p. 92). In view of his fulsome praise of *Irene* and the remark that Johnson's "prose is often the most exquisite poetry," it was perhaps just as well that he slighted Johnson's other poems (p. 93). In *Irene*, "L" discovered the required observation of the unities and a style "nervous, sentimental, and poetical." He made no mention of the play's faults, although he indicated that it had failed on the stage.[3]

Like some of the other biographers, "L" ignored the rest of Johnson's poetry in order to concentrate on his prose works, but paid scant attention to the *Idler*, the *Journey to the Western Islands*, and, what is more odd, the *Dictionary*, which had been almost universally acclaimed at the time as Johnson's greatest effort.[4] The *Journey* he compared briefly to the account of the well-known antiquary, Thomas Pennant, and was quick to remark that the object of Johnson's travels was not to observe nature, but to study men and manners. He found similar virtues in the *Rambler* and *Rasselas*. "L" slighted the moral aspects of these works to focus on the "noble excursions of Fancy" in the *Rambler*, especially in the Eastern tales (p. 94), and on Johnson's capturing the "sublimity of the Eastern manner of expression" and the "fertility of invention" in *Rasselas* (pp. 95–96).[5] In addition, "L" opposed those who argued that the style of the *Rambler* was too correct and heavy-handed, but instead of proving his point, he quoted at great length from Vicesimus Knox's appraisal of Johnson's style (p. 94). Brief as it was, "L's" criticism of these two works is interesting

25

because he was not preoccupied with their moral themes. His concern, such as it was, was focused almost exclusively on the creative aspects of these writings.

It was in his discussions of Johnson's political pamphlets and the *Lives* that "L's" hero-worship was most evident. In both cases, he maintained, Johnson descended from the hero's pedestal to endanger his hard-won reputation. Johnson's belief in apparitions, according to "L," rendered him fair game for literary snipers like Churchill; but even worse was Johnson's descent into the pit of political pamphleteering, which "L" likened to Jupiter's stooping to combat the gladiators. This biographer, however, defended Johnson's political works, to each of which he gave a one-sentence summary, saying that if Johnson's sentiments were "obnoxious," they were at least consistently so (pp. 96–97).

Curiously enough, in view of his encomiastic attitude to Johnson's works, "L" mounted one of the most outspoken contemporary attacks on Johnson's prejudices in the *Lives*. He centered on the biography of Milton, but it was obvious that he deeply regretted the damage done to Johnson's reputation:

> But when we anticipate the lustre
> with which the name of Johnson
> will shine amongst our descendants,
> it is impossible to read such senti-
> ments without a regret not abso-
> lutely devoid of indignation (p. 97).

26

Here, as with Johnson's credulity and political writings, "L" thought that Johnson had recklessly undermined his own position as a literary hero. Thus, despite his protests to the contrary at the beginning of the *Memoirs,* the author in fact presented Johnson as a hero who unfortunately could not hide his essential humanity in his works. "L's" defense of Johnson was weak precisely because he excused him for the human qualities which would have required no excuse unless he took Johnson for a hero rather than a man. In other words, "L" compromised his own position as a biographer by first promising to show Johnson in his true colors, and then regretting, somewhat bitterly, that Johnson displayed these colors in some of his works.

The most valuable service which "L" performed, a service largely ignored, was his identification of several of Johnson's works. The Johnson canon, still receiving additions today, began to take shape in his own lifetime, and his early biographers contributed in no small way to its formulation.[6] No particular biographer (nor the early biographers collectively), however, identified the entire Johnson canon. Furthermore, even in those biographies concerned almost exclusively with Johnson the writer, there was no systematic attempt to define the canon with accuracy, though there were surprisingly few wrong attributions made. In these biographies, the usual procedure was to describe in detail the main works which everyone knew were Johnson's and to lump the minor pieces together, sometimes without individual titles.

More important, the successive biographical appraisals of Johnson's writings indicated a steady growth in the knowledge of and interest in Johnson's works. Noteworthy, too, was the fact that the efforts to establish his canon were made in the face of many difficulties, chief among them Johnson's recourse to anonymity, which led him to put his name to only twelve works.[7] Moreover, Johnson was never fond of identifying his earlier productions.

In his study of the canon, Donald Greene overlooks the *Memoirs*. In the first place, Greene maintains that Johnson's work on the Parliamentary Debates for the *Gentleman's Magazine* and on the *Adventurer* was probably not known in his lifetime.[8] But "L's" account, published while Johnson was still alive, mentioned Johnson's contributions to both, even listing in a note Johnson's contributions to the *Adventurer*, accounting for all but four of his pieces (pp. 92, 94).

Similarly, Greene indicates that the first attribution of Johnson's translation of part of Father Sarpi's *History of the Council of Trent* (1738) was made by Tyers. Actually, "L" ascribed this work to Johnson four months before Tyers did, and lamented that Johnson did not complete the translation (p. 92). Greene also assigns to Tyers the first ascription of Johnson's preface to Anna Williams's *Miscellanies* (1766). Greene, in this connection, is partly correct, for although "L" observed that Johnson contributed some pieces to the Williams volume, he did not specify the preface (p. 97). "L," therefore, deserves more recognition than he has received for identifying some of Johnson's productions.

Near the end of the *Memoirs,* "L" unceremoniously jerked the reader from Johnson's literary career back to his biography when he made a brief mention of Johnson's marriage. This insertion was not only a violation of the chronological plan "L" adopted, but it demonstrated how clumsily biography and criticism were sometimes united in the eighteenth century. No effort was made to connect Johnson's marriage with his writings, and the account seemed to have been inserted for its own sake, with no logical relation to what preceded or followed it. As we shall see, this incoherence was a feature of several other lives.

II

The next biography to center on Johnson as writer was *An Account of the Writings of Dr. Samuel Johnson, including Incidents of his Life,* published in the *European Magazine.*[9] Austin Dobson describes it as little more than laborious, undistinguished journalism, yet Donald Greene finds it a "most competent account of Johnson's writing," and seems surprised at the neglect of this "particularly striking" essay.[10] Both critics are, in fact, correct in their appraisals of this anonymous work. As biography, this essay is virtually negligible; as an account of Johnson's works, it is of great value.

The *Account* ignored biographical considerations

in order to concentrate on a long descriptive list of Johnson's writings. Moreover, since the first install-ment of the article appeared in the same month as Johnson's death, it is obvious that such hasty publica-tion demanded almost exclusive attention to the canon and to the few biographical facts generally known.

This biographer was well aware of the limitations imposed on his essay. Acknowledging Johnson as a public figure open to abundant curiosity, he indicated that several biographies were forthcoming; therefore, his endeavor, as he saw it, was a contribution to bi-ographical material rather than a biography complete in itself. As such it could assist future biographers of Johnson. He amplified his position by cautioning later biographers who deal in "petty peculiarities" to dis-charge their task with "that discretion which candour, we hope, will dictate to them on a subject of so much delicacy" (p. 411). Although in theory he was on the side of discreet biography, this biographer, in offering a mere compilation of Johnson's works, ignored the is-sue of decorum in practice. His position on this matter bore on two fundamental questions in biography: first, this author (at least for his own purposes) divorced bi-ography from criticism by the near elimination of biographical data; second, in his comment that "the character of a man of letters will . . . be best known by his writings" (p. 411), he revealed his belief that a writer's life was his writing. Nothing apart from his works was truly valuable.

The only biographical portion of the *Account* described Johnson's pre-London days, and, as usual, the materials were scanty, the bulk of them covered by printing the Walmesley and Gower letters of recommendation for Johnson. This author, however, advanced a view different from that of "L" regarding Johnson's career. Whereas "L" staunchly maintained that Johnson's genius was powerful enough to have overcome the obscurity of country life had he been destined to it, the biographer of the *European Magazine* felt otherwise. He was grateful that Gower's letter failed. Had Gower succeeded, he wrote, "it is probable [Johnson] would have sunk into obscurity, and passed the rest of his life merely as the Head of a Provincial Academy" (p. 413).

Only three other biographical anecdotes interrupted this writer's list of Johnson's writings, and two — Johnson's altercations with Thomas Osborne and Chesterfield — were in no way dramatized through the inclusion of detail. The third, dealing with Johnson's appeal to Smollett to obtain Francis Barber's release from conscription in the navy, included Smollett's caustic letter to John Wilkes on Barber's behalf.[11] In refusing to dramatize or speculate on these incidents, this author sustained his objective approach, although with some cost to liveliness. The only crack in his facade of objectivity occurred when he stoutly defended Johnson's acceptance of his pension. It is difficult to reprimand the writer of the *Account* on this point, for it is clear that his aim was to avoid stressing biographical incidents no matter how colorful or revealing they were, and he was true to his conceived image of Johnson.

It was in his long account of Johnson's works that this biographer made his real contribution to Johnsoniana. His was not a critical biography, although he included brief critical comments from time to time. Usually he was content to identify the work and its date. As did most of his contemporaries, he considered the *Dictionary* the "most laborious and important of [Johnson's] works" (p. 10), and gave a brief account of its reception (pp. 81–82). He called the Drury Lane Prologue "the most perfect performance in that species of composition" (p. 11), and underplayed the failure of *Irene*, merely indicating that the play was not successful despite the adept performances of the actors (p. 11). The only work with which he quarreled, and in this opinion he followed the strictures of most of his contemporaries, was the edition of Shakespeare, where he criticized Johnson's failure to fulfill his plan of reading the books that Shakespeare presumably had read (p. 83). These are the only works about which this biographer had much to say; thus as a guide to the contemporary attitude towards Johnson's writing this essay contributed little, nor, for that matter, was it intended to do so.

While not by any means a scholarly biography, the *Account* nevertheless demonstrated a scholarly care and perception not often found in the early biographies of Johnson. Footnote references to periodicals, pamphlets, county histories, and Johnson's work abounded, as did quotations from Johnson and other writers. This author was usually careful to cite his sources of information; for instance, he was the first writer who attributed to Johnson the *Complete Vindication of the Licensers of the Stage* (1739) "on the authority of an old bookseller who remembered the publication of it" (p. 9).[12]

Additional evidence of his common sense may be found in his careful guesses and conclusions. He did not state facts as certainties unless he was absolutely convinced of their authenticity. Compared to some of the other biographers, this biographer's care was rather striking. He corrected the erroneous attribution to Johnson of the Epilogue spoken at the opening of Drury Lane (p. 11). The ascriptions of the translation of Fontenelle's panegyric on Dr. Louis Morin (1742), of the life of Nicholas Rienzi (p. 11), and the preface to Sir Walter Raleigh's *The Interest of England with Regard to Foreign Alliances Explained* (1750) (p. 81) he questioned seriously without denying them as Johnson's, and in the last two cases his suspicions were well-founded.[13] He also refused to offer a definite reason for Johnson's quitting Oxford, and instead posed two alternatives — the expense involved in continuing his studies or Johnson's dislike of the university — and tentatively chose the first because it was "generally supposed to have been the case" (p. 411). He indirectly corrected "L's" assertion that Cave had cheated Johnson on the income from *London* by saying that had Cave been guilty, Johnson would hardly have written his biography (p. 413). He saw the value of seemingly trivial documents, and was the first biographer to reprint Johnson's letter in praise of Milton published in the *General Advertiser* on 4 April 1750, the day before the benefit for Milton's granddaughter (pp. 11–12). He included the letter because, as he said, it was "little known, and liable to be lost in a newspaper" (p. 11).

Despite his care, this biographer's presentation was not flawless, even within its own self-imposed limitations. As Greene notes, he made several attributions to Johnson for the first time: in fact, Greene's list credits this author with more attributions to the Johnson canon than any other writer before Boswell, including Hawkins.[14] But he made incorrect ascriptions as well. He credited Johnson with all of the Parliamentary Debates written after 1744, but we now know that Hawkesworth succeeded Johnson in this project. He erroneously assigned to Johnson the "Life of Chaucer," "Reflections on the State of Portugal," and "An Essay on Architecture," (p. 83), all for the *Universal Visitor*.[15] Furthermore, he denied Johnson's authorship of the "Epitaph on Claudy Philips," which he incorrectly attributed to Garrick (p. 9).

Since almost any detailed description of a work or an incident in a biography so brief as this one seems overstressed, it may seem unfair to charge the author with imbalance. However, curious instances of imbalance do exist in the *Account*. The biographer, for example, reprinted Johnson's early poem, *Ad Urba-*

num, in Latin yet devoted only two sentences to *London.* One wonders, too, why he included such a long footnote recounting the life of Zachariah Williams, father of Anna Williams (pp. 82–83). The note itself has little connection with the fact that, as the author mentioned, Johnson wrote for Zachariah Williams *An Account of an Attempt to Ascertain the Longitude at Sea.* In light of his normally judicious use of footnotes, this lengthy and irrelevant one is jarring in context.

Taken together, the *Memoirs* and the *Account* were slight, both in scope and in original information about Johnson's life. They provided no startling new biographical details, but in identifying a considerable portion of the Johnson canon, even without venturing to sit in judgment on his works, they performed the first task of any biographer who writes the life of an author. To those interested in the Johnson canon, these two essays are clearly required reading.

As biography, these two articles are the most marginal to be considered. They made no sustained attempts to relate his work to his life, and furnished no insights into the workings of his mind, the nature of his personality, and of his relationships with others. But they did project an image of Johnson as a writer whose works deserved identification and recognition.

III

Shortly after the death of Tom Davies on 5 May 1785, there appeared an anonymous octavo volume of

197 pages entitled *Memoirs of the Life and Writings of the Late Dr. Samuel Johnson,* a work by William Shaw (1749–1831), Gaelic scholar and dissenting minister.[16] Of all the early biographers of Johnson with the exception of Tyers, Shaw is the least worthy of the neglect he has received. Shaw's was the first critical biography of Johnson, and although it contained more purely biographical information than the two accounts previously examined, biographical elements were subsidiary to his treatment of Johnson's writings. To be sure, this piece was uneven in its distribution of space and criticism of some of Johnson's writings, and it occasionally suffered from patches of incoherence and feeble efforts to imitate Johnson's style, but judged as a whole, especially in view of the haste with which it was written and published, the *Memoirs* is a commendable biography.

Shaw began by paying homage to Johnson as a figure whose "virtuous intelligence" made him worthy of commemoration (pp. 3–6). In accordance with the conventional notion of biographical utility, Shaw declared that Johnson was an unexcelled example of the man of letters who inspired his contemporaries to "exertion and perseverance in virtue or excellence" and who would inspire posterity to contemplate and emulate his moral and literary merits (p. 4). Consequently, Shaw gave as the rationale for writing Johnson's biography the necessary preservation of his moral and literary fame, and also the stimulation of future biographies:

His transcendent abilities, and tried
virtues, his oddities, which were
alike original and abundant; the variety of his friends, and the length
of his life, give so many shapes to his
story, and such different complex-
ions to the prompt and occasional
ebullitions of his wit in different
situations, that whoever had the
honour of his acquaintance must be
in possession of materials which, for
the sake of literature and posterity,
ought to be recorded (pp. 5–6).

Early in the *Memoirs,* Shaw took great pains to
prove that he was qualified to be Johnson's biographer.
As shown in the passage just quoted, Shaw was well
aware of the scarcity of factual information about
Johnson, particularly concerning his youth. Indeed,
he was perhaps too skeptical of the possible discovery of
any details of Johnson's pre-London days: "The anecdotes of his juvenile days have perished with the companions of his youth. Few interest themselves in the
history of a man without property, fame or consequence" (p. 2).[17] Twice, when he dealt with the failure
of Johnson's boarding school (p. 26) and when he
could rot explain how Johnson and Cave became
friends (p. 37), he cited the lack of documented evidence for his inability to present the circumstances
fully. Therefore, in a brief "Preface," he was quick to

disclose his main sources of information, particularly the late Tom Davies and James Elphinston, and he continually referred to his sources, many of whom he left unidentified, in order to support his claim to authenticity. Given the absence of such data, Shaw wisely resisted the temptation to state as fact what was uncertain. For instance, he attacked the notion that Johnson left Oxford prematurely because he disobeyed the rules and treated the instructors with disdain. He refused to believe this tale because it was unsupported by authority and it did not fit the "tenor" of Johnson's behavior as a mature man (pp. 17–18). This habit of judging a man's juvenile conduct by that of his adult years is, of course, dangerous, even though it argues that Shaw, unlike most of his rival biographers, was alive to the relationship between a man's youth and adulthood.

But like other biographers, he could not withstand the impulse to speculate on the nature of Johnson's career had he remained to graduate from Oxford, and like "L" he cautiously advanced the notion that the tenor of Johnson's early life would not have halted the growth of his genius (pp. 19–20). At the same time, he was forced to admit that the pressures of necessity had a salutary effect on Johnson's willingness to endure the labor of authorship:

> Johnson . . . immersed in a school might have published less, but except he had written much, he could

not, with all the advantages of leisure, retirement, and plenty, have
written so well as he did, amidst the
incessant bustle of a town life, exposed to the constant intrusions of
the idle and officious, and precipi-
tated by the frequent pressure of impending want (pp. 20–21).

Shaw, moreover, exercised restraint in exploring
Johnson's motives and actions. His treatment of Johnson's precocity was carefully, if briefly, presented; it
was solid rather than flashy. Shaw was careful to stress
that the reasons for Johnson's removal to London were
probable, not certain: "This adventure was not perhaps so much the consequence of disappointed expectations, as of his strong propensity for literary pur-
suits" (p. 27). His care was also demonstrated in his
quietly stated disbelief that Johnson dashed off the
Life of Savage in thirty-six hours (p. 44).

Because he saw the difficulty of securing the information necessary for a full portrait of his subject,
Shaw, like the biographer of the *European Magazine,*
kept his eye open for the smallest shreds of useful detail. Confessing, for instance, his inability to account
for Johnson's abandonment of the translation of Sarpi's *History of the Council of Trent,* he begged that
the few sheets of the translation which might have been
preserved be brought to light, for "the public will be
highly indebted to the editor, who shall be the first to

present it with such an acceptable curiosity" (pp. 44–45).

The most valuable part of Shaw's study of the *Rambler* was his scholarly description of James Elphinston's reprinting of the *Rambler* in Scotland. Shaw doubtless felt that he was paying a debt to Elphinston by mentioning his work, for Elphinston not only supplied him with material for the *Memoirs,* but had introduced him to Johnson. Furthermore, Shaw published for the first time four of Johnson's letters to Elphinston which indicated his deep regard for the Scot.[18] The entire account was, of course, original, and served to reveal Shaw's attention to background information valuable as a picture of the behind-the-scenes activity in publishing.

For all his care in sifting and presenting evidence, Shaw made some inexcusable mistakes. He misdated two of Johnson's most admired works, *The Vanity of Human Wishes,* which he assigned to 1759 instead of 1749 (p. 61), and the *Plan of the Dictionary,* whose date he missed by a few months (p. 76). In addition, perhaps in his desire to make Johnson something of a hero, he opened his biography by remarking that Johnson had outlived all of his earlier acquaintances and most of his later friends. This was hardly the truth. Although he survived such close friends as Anna Williams, Robert Levett, and Henry Thrale, many of his intimate associates — Mrs. Thrale, Fanny Burney, Boswell, Hawkins, Reynolds, Burke and Murphy — survived him, some by several years. In his endeavor to portray Johnson's literary accomplishments as heroic triumphs over bitter conditions and the cruel indifference of his betters, Shaw sometimes exaggerated, as when he adduced Johnson's habit of rolling his head as he read as proof of his unremitting pursuit of knowledge when young (pp. 13–14), or when he maintained that many of the anecdotes later used by Johnson in the *Lives* were first heard when he worked in his father's bookstore (pp. 15–16). Generally speaking, however, the *Memoirs* was free from serious factual errors and perpetuated no misinterpretations of Johnson's character.

Although not psychologically oriented, Shaw's biography cast occasional glimpses at the relationship between Johnson's character and his writings. He was not the only biographer to do so, but the care with which he advanced psychological speculations was noteworthy. Despite its brevity, the account of Johnson's productions as the response to necessity rather than to leisurely choice was worthwhile, and was occasionally repeated throughout the *Memoirs,* especially in regard to the depressing conditions under which Johnson compiled the *Dictionary* and his frequent attempts at refuge from bouts of melancholy in the society of friends. Likewise, Shaw treated the inevitable clash between Johnson's rude appearance and gruff manners on one hand, and his profound intelligence and pointed wit on the other with a curious mixture of awe and the confidence that it was his declared mission to defend Johnson from those whose estimate of genius was based on appearance and grace. Shaw, in addition, was one of the few biographers to recognize the importance of Johnson's genealogy, about which little was known by Johnson's contemporaries. Shaw made no effort to trace Michael Johnson's influence on his son, although his brief portrait flattered Michael. Shaw managed, however, a witty aside on Johnson's relationship with his father:

> His intellectual abilities unimproved and called forth by new interest or emergency, were notwithstanding perhaps but moderate, as it does not follow, that because the son made a figure, the father should be a prodigy (p. 9).

Shaw likewise treated Johnson's marriage in little detail, and the picture he painted was somewhat prettier than warranted. His account of Johnson's grief after Tetty's death is one of the most poignant descriptions of Johnson's sorrow.

On the whole, however, Shaw was very reticent when dealing with Johnson's melancholy temperament and self-deprecation partly, it seems, owing to the lack of material and partly because he obeyed the dictates of discreet biography.

Most of Shaw's work was devoted to Johnson the writer, and it is to this element that we now turn. He organized the critical section of the *Memoirs* chronologically, with no attempt to order his discussion on the moral themes or structural similarities of Johnson's writings. It is clear that Johnson's "secular" works constituted the main appeal for Shaw, because those works to which he gave extended commentary were not the moral writings such as *Rasselas,* the *Rambler,* and the *Idler.*

Shaw began his study of Johnson with a glimpse at literary conditions in London in general and in Grub Street in particular. He described London as a place of opportunity for an enterprising, industrious young writer on one hand, and a literary market overrun by knaves and swindlers on the other. Because Shaw, like most of his contemporaries, felt that Johnson's Grub-Street days cast a shadow on his reputation, he was reluctant to discuss the "petit pieces" Johnson turned out for the *Gentleman's Magazine,* admitting only that some of them were "excelled by nothing he has since produced" (pp. 37–38). Shaw recognized, too, the difficulty of identifying Johnson's early work:

> It is impossible to be exact in stating the dates of these publications, or giving the history of their origin and composition. The particulars they involve are the less interesting, that they seem to have grown into request only since the fame of the author has been established; that they are distinguished by no other species

of excellence than fidelity and per-
spicuity, and they might still have
continued unadmired, and even unknown, but for the superior lustre of
subsequent performances (pp. 72–
73).

Shaw's perceptive comments on the effect an author's
fame had on his earlier works which would otherwise
be consigned to oblivion were unparalleled in any
other biography of Johnson. The distinction he made
between sincere admiration and retroactive approval
revealed his awareness of the shifts in literary reputation. He was not dazzled by Johnson's fame into excessive praise of his earlier work. Despite his obvious concern for the Johnson canon, Shaw added only one
item—the preface to James Fordyce's *Sermons to
Young Women* (p. 143).[19]

Few of Johnson's contemporaries valued his poetry
highly, and Shaw was no exception to the prevailing
opinion. He reprinted *Ad Urbanum* in its entirety followed by a translation of an anonymous friend (pp.
34–37), but failed to comment on this, Johnson's first
work for Cave. When Shaw proceeded to Johnson's two
greatest poems, he lapsed into cheap personal bias. Although he commended *London* as an "elegant and
masterly production" (p. 46) and recounted the stock
anecdote of Pope's praise of the poem, most of his remarks were unfavorable. He made the subtle charge
that Johnson, for some unexplained reason, conceived

a perpetual dislike for Pope which found expression in his criticism of Pope's poetry. Shaw then turned Johnson's strictures on Pope's Horatian imitations on *London* and incorporated detailed criticism of some of Johnson's lines written by an anonymous friend, possibly Thomas Morris, who just happened to be an admirer of Pope. For the most part, this criticism was mere "nit-picking" designed to repay Johnson by proving him guilty of the same poetic faults which he had detected in the poetry of Pope and Addison.[20] Although his criticism of *London* was over-literal and certainly questionable, Shaw supplied a valuable account of Johnson's state of mind at the time he wrote the poem. He briefly traced the differences between Johnson's accustomed life in the provinces and the distress of that in London. Shaw's comment is worth quoting as a sort of rudimentary exploration of the relation of an author's mind to his work:

> This poem, very probably, gives an exact picture of *London,* as it appeared to his mind immediately on his leaving the country, while every rural convenience was yet recollected with regret, and those of the town had been enjoyed only to such a degree, in such company, or under such circumstances, as might rather disgust than gratify. The difficulty of securing a prospect of employment,

before he could be known, the shy-
ness of the booksellers, to interest
themselves in the fortune or business of a stranger, the wants of fu-
turity which could hope but little
assistance from the present, which
was unequal to its own supply, ill
health, few friends, exquisite sensi-
bility, and a temper of mind, rather
melancholy than chearful, obviously
account for the indignant spirit, and
strong assemblage of melancholy
imagery with which that performance abounds (pp. 54–55).

Although this statement clashed with Johnson's frequent protests of intense love for London's gaiety, bustle, and opportunities, it seemed a reasonable assertion,
and considering the almost complete neglect of such
speculation in the other biographies of Johnson, it is
tempting to call Shaw a pioneer of sorts.

Shaw's strictures on *The Vanity of Human Wishes*
were similar to this on *London*. He drew invidious
comparisons between Johnson's imitation of Juvenal
and that by Thomas Morris, published shortly before
Shaw's life, and which Shaw puffed in a footnote.
Shaw, failing to recognize Johnson's desire for independence from the original, took him to task for not
imitating Juvenal more literally.

More forcefully than any other biographer, Shaw
scored Johnson's poetry:

His poetry, though not any where loaded with epithets, is destitute of animation. The strong sense, the biting sarcasm, the deep solemnity, which mark his genius, no where assumes that union, symmetry, or collected energy, which is necessary to produce a general effect. We are now and then struck with a fine thought, a fine line, or a fine passage, but little interested by the whole. His mode of versifying, which is an imitation of Pope, may bear analization [sic], but after reading his best pieces once, few are desirous of reading them again (pp. 71–72).

The strong emotional quality of Johnson's verse, for which it is now prized, was lost on Shaw, who, unable to discover in Johnson's poetry the same intellectual vigor he valued in his prose, could only condemn it.[21]

His position on Johnson's poetry was all the more curious in view of his treatment of *Irene*. Shaw was too partial to this work to criticize it; for example, he refused to attribute its failure to Johnson's weakness in writing appealing drama. Rather, he preferred to blame the audience for unrefined taste and defended Johnson's persistent refusal to pander to Garrick in order to insure the play's success. Shaw implicitly blamed Garrick for the play's failure, and his final judgment was most irresponsible: "And though Garrick was of the party, posterity who shall mourn *Irene*, will be rather apt to impute her fate to inanimate acting, than unskilful writing" (pp. 86–87).

Shaw's antipathy to the taste of the English public prompted him to assign to Johnson a more contentious motive for undertaking the *Rambler* than was the case. Johnson was not, as Shaw maintained, contemptuous of English taste, although he admittedly sought to refine it in the *Rambler* essays. Again, Shaw blamed the public for the tepid reception of the *Rambler* and made a pointless comparison between Johnson, who labored with gnawing inconvenience, and Hume, a gentleman author whose seemingly effortless success offended him.

In his discussion of the *Idler* which, incidentally, he preferred to the *Rambler,* Shaw was careful to point out that the *Idler* was not conceived as a sequel to the *Rambler.* He especially admired Johnson's originality and variety of subject matter in the *Idler,* as well as his sustained point of view, a quality which few modern critics would assign it. Oddly enough, Shaw made no mention of its lighter tone by which it was — and is — usually distinguished from the *Rambler.* But the greatest appeal of the *Idler* for Shaw was its openness, its obvious embodiment of Johnson's own feelings and foibles in fictional characters.

Like other biographers, Shaw was impressed with Johnson's oriental pieces. He used Johnson's translation of Lobo's *Voyage to Abyssinia* to show Johnson's youthful facility in capturing the "tropical language of the Orientals" (p. 129). Shaw defended him from the charges of an overwrought style and employed a quotation from Johnson's preface to Lobo to prove how original were his plan of composition and his mode of thought (pp. 130–33). But his main concern was the relation of the translation to *Rasselas*, Johnson's most sustained oriental composition. Strangely, he omitted any critical remarks on the novel, but he argued that *Rasselas* perhaps had been planned about the same time that Johnson worked on Lobo. This revealed that Shaw, unlike most of the other biographers, had some sense of the interrelationship of Johnson's works.

Shaw devoted more space than any other biographer to Johnson's *Debates in the Senate of Lilliput*, written for the *Gentleman's Magazine*. Partly owing to the contemporary notion that Johnson was a rockbound Tory, Shaw mistakenly asserted that Johnson wrote these articles as a gesture of contempt for the House of Commons. But Shaw, in describing the circumstances of Johnson's composition of these fabrications, portrayed Johnson as the literary hero triumphant over drudgery and depression. Johnson achieved success in the debates despite ill health, and, as indicated by the "form of his alphabet, which inclines strongly to the left, instead of the right," he wrote with a tired hand (p. 42). On the whole, Shaw's estimate of the Parliamentary Debates was balanced and judicious, although his contention, advanced later by Boswell and Birkbeck Hill, that Johnson did not discriminate between the speakers has been recently disproved.[22]

In affirming that Johnson's other political writings revealed "solid reasoning and sound information," Shaw stood almost alone among his contemporaries (p. 122). Whereas other biographers argued that Johnson's role as a hero was irreparably damaged by his fall into the quagmire of political pamphleteering, Shaw approved Johnson's literary mingling with the politicians. If, in Shaw's mind, Johnson's artistry and genius were fully evident in such pamphlets, there was no logical reason why he should be attacked for them, at least on a literary basis. He gave unstinting praise to Johnson's *An Introduction to the Political State of Great Britain* and *Observations on the State of Affairs* (1756), and his approval of the more notable pamphlets of the seventies was even more emphatic. It must be made clear, however, that Shaw's defense of the political writings, made in full knowledge of the abuse to which Johnson's views were subjected, was rendered solely in literary, rather than political, terms. He commended the pamphlets not for their political acumen but for the "promptitude of invention, that ardour of genius, that brilliancy of imagination, and that energy of expression which characterise his writings" (p. 142). Ultimately, Shaw's applause of the pamphlets rang too loud; his prophecy that Johnson's tracts would be read long after the events which occasioned them had been forgotten was certainly inaccurate. Nevertheless, because his forceful defense of these works was nearly unique in the late eighteenth century, Shaw's remarks deserve notice.

Shaw offered surprisingly little comment on Johnson's criticism, which was at the time discussed more widely than any other aspect of his writings. He merely mentioned the publication of the *Miscellaneous Observations on the Tragedy of Macbeth* (1745), and then only to show Johnson's cordial treatment of William Warburton, whose edition of Shakespeare appeared two years later. He spent more time, however, with the *Proposals* for the edition of Shakespeare than did most other biographers, and quoted extensively from it (pp. 124–26). In addition, he devoted more space to the edition itself, bestowing special praise on Johnson's virtues as an editor:

> His notes in various parts of the work, his explanation of difficult passages, his development of hidden beauties, his interpretations of obscurities, and his candour and ingenuity in reconciling inconsistencies, discover no superficial acquaintance with either men or books (p. 138).

Though brief, Shaw's observation on the *Lives of the Poets* was a reliable index to the contemporary reception of Johnson as a critic. After providing a short account of the negotiations between Johnson and the booksellers regarding this project, Shaw, following his tendency to emphasize the heroic proportions of Johnson's labor, marvelled at his perseverance and vigor at such an advanced age. Shaw granted unqualified approval to the *Lives,* reserving special praise for those of Cowley, Dryden, and that portion of Milton which dealt with *Paradise Lost.* Shaw gave no over-view of the *Lives,* nor did he discuss the controversial biographies. He was content, on the contrary, to pass a general evaluation of the significance of the *Lives* as "giving at once stability to our tongue, and formation to our taste," thereby constructing a firm basis for Johnson's fame as a critic (pp. 172–73).

Despite frequent and vigorous attacks on his critical prejudices, Johnson was widely esteemed as a critic in his own day. It was, however, his *Dictionary* which won almost universal acclaim as his masterpiece. To Shaw, the *Plan of a Dictionary* (1747) was the instrument by which Johnson achieved fame for the first time, helped, of course, by the promised assistance of Chesterfield (pp. 76–77). Shaw's estimate of the *Plan* was one of his most balanced pronouncements. "It will not be denied," he wrote,

> that [Johnson] possesses more energy of language, and perhaps a more beautiful arrangement of the multifarious particulars to which he solicits the public attention, but he certainly wants the simplicity, and indeed is proscribed by his subject

from displaying the knowledge, of Chambers (p. 79).

What Shaw prized above all in Johnson's proposal was the "utility in the aim, and originality in the execution" (p. 79), and the patience, industry, and discrimination which Johnson brought to his task (pp. 81–82). Shaw, unfortunately, could not forbear riding his hobby horse, and in his treatment both of the *Plan* and of the *Dictionary,* he vigorously repeated his sentimental assertion of Johnson's Herculean effort in the face of poverty and ill health (pp. 81, 106–7). Given his penchant for emphasizing the depressing conditions under which Johnson was often forced to labor, Shaw's diatribe against Chesterfield's alleged neglect was not unexpected. And, as always, Shaw's indignation was based on Johnson's later fame:

> It is a disgrace to his memory, and to the age, that the author of an undertaking so arduous and extensive was not placed beyond the recurrence of necessity, and that while his genius was conferring permanency on their language, the exigencies of his situation impelled him to apply to other means for daily subsistence (p. 80).

Generally, Shaw's comment on the *Dictionary* was astute. His description of the book's reception is valuable (pp. 115–19). Many of his contemporaries objected to some of the prejudiced definitions, but these Shaw excused, saying that certain definitions in a work of such scope were bound to arouse ill-feeling. Although Shaw was an avid student of language, his criticism of the *Dictionary* was refreshingly non-technical; when Shaw cited examples of particular definitions he refrained from a study of such elements as etymology and orthography.

The only other major work Shaw examined was the *Journey to the Western Islands.* Here he repeated the conventional praise of Johnson's attention to men and manners and his satirical jibes. But Shaw's main concern for this work was its role in the famous Ossian controversy, a controversy in which Shaw, as a linguist, was intensely interested. Shaw was no idle adventurer in this matter, for he possessed eminent qualifications. He had written *An Analysis of the Galic Language* (1778), a work of which Johnson approved.[23] Johnson and Boswell subscribed to his *Galic and English Dictionary* (1780), and Johnson had contributed moral and critical support to this undertaking.[24] Indeed, according to Shaw, it was Johnson who gave him the greatest encouragement. " 'Sir,' said Johnson:

> if you would give the world a Vocabulary of that language, while the island of Great-Britain stands in the Atlantic Ocean, your name will be mentioned.' By such a speech, and from such a man, the youthful mind

of Shaw went with ardour in pursuit of the objects in question. He
performed a journey of 3000 miles,
persevered and finished his work at
his own expense . . . (pp. 153–54).

The curious element in Shaw's account of the Ossian affair was his objective self-introduction: "About
Christmas, 1774, the Rev. Mr. Shaw was introduced to
Johnson, by the kind offices of Mr. Elphinston" (p.
148). If this was an effort to insure anonymity, it was
an obvious failure, since the eighteen pages which
Shaw gave to his own presence in Johnson's life was his
most intimate and detailed account of Johnson's relationships with any individual. This is not to say that
Shaw's account was dramatic — it was not; he recorded
few conversations and printed for the first time only
one of Johnson's letters of recommendation for him
(pp. 156–57).[25]

Although at times, as when Shaw repeated Johnson's praise of him (pp. 149, 151, 153–54), this inter-
lude appeared as a mere instrument of self-aggrandize-
ment, it was carefully fitted into the account of the
Ossian controversy.[26] Shaw was one of the principal
figures in this debate, siding with Johnson against the
authenticity of Macpherson's poems, and printing
Johnson's famous letter charging the impostor with
fraud.

Shaw plunged into the controversy with a pamphlet
entitled *An Enquiry into the Authenticity of the Po-*

ems Ascribed to Ossian (1781), and there followed an exchange of pamphlets with John Clark of Edinburgh.[27] Johnson aided Shaw with his second tract, although in the biography Shaw did not acknowledge his help. Shaw's main contribution in the *Memoirs* was his reprinting of a letter to Johnson by "Anti-Ossian" begging Johnson to help Shaw carry on the struggle against Clark (pp. 159–65). Shaw then announced that Johnson had intended to furnish a long account of the Ossian debate, but owing to poor health, he never wrote it.

This episode, with racy, intimate detail, seems curiously out of place with the rest of the *Memoirs*. But, although the fabric of his account of the Ossian debate is of an altogether different texture from that of the remainder of the *Memoirs*, it is woven closely enough with the rest of the essay so that its jarring effect is minimal. It is, besides, a vivid account of a famous incident in Johnson's life, and serves to illustrate the entirely different quality of biography when written with a sense of communion with the subject. The importance of acquaintance with the subject, both in terms of factual information and confidence of approach, is underscored in this section of the *Memoirs*.

The concluding portion of the *Memoirs* was a tasteful description of Johnson's final years. Since he concentrated largely on Johnson the writer, Shaw did not mention any possible objections to the reprinting of many of Johnson's letters, even when he included Johnson's letter to Elphinston on the death of Elphinston's mother, a letter whose tenderness and commiseration might have stimulated cries of the invasion of privacy. Similarly, he mentioned the recurrent accounts of Johnson's decline, but regretted their "minute and tiresome exactness" less on moral than on literary grounds (p. 173). He then proceeded to give his own account with taste and moderation (pp. 173–84), again deploring the indifference shown to Johnson in his lifetime. Unlike other biographers, he treated the delicate subject of Mrs. Thrale's marriage to Gabriel Piozzi and its effect on Johnson with tact and moderation, though he made clear Johnson's keen disappointment over the marriage. And like almost everyone else, he pictured Johnson's as a model Christian death.

Moreover, Shaw obeyed tradition by concluding with a conventional character sketch in which he cursorily surveyed Johnson's sense of wit and humor, his conversational habits, and his idiosyncrasies. None of these Shaw amplified with dramatic illustrations, for he was skeptical of the value of the endless proliferation of Johnsonian anecdotes.

Although Shaw held Johnson in high regard as a man, it was chiefly as a writer that Johnson appealed to him. Shaw never tired of extolling Johnson's originality of thought and expression, his "sagacious, discriminating, and well-informed mind," a mind, he said, "manured in learning" (pp. 186, 187). But to Shaw the most attractive element of Johnson's career was that he continued to write even after his pension had made him independent of writing as a livelihood.

This was precisely why Shaw could defend Johnson's acceptance of his pension. Shaw, as mentioned earlier, had described Hume as a gentleman author who never knew what it was to live from day to day strictly on the scanty resources of literary productivity. That the quality of Johnson's writing did not decline after he was granted the pension was a source of gratification to Shaw, and was, in his own mind, the principal attribute of Johnson's greatness.

IV

Another interesting examination of Johnson's works was *An Essay on the Life, Character, and Writings of Dr. Samuel Johnson,* written by Dr. Joseph Towers (1737–1799), and published by Charles Dilly in 1786.[28] In several respects, Towers's life, as Walter Raleigh points out, was quite similar to Johnson's: they were sons of booksellers, raised in non-affluent circumstances, and acquainted with Latin and Greek. Both sought their fortunes in London, both were engaged in vast literary projects, chiefly biography (Towers's best work is his two-volume life of Frederick the Third), and both received the degree of Doctor of Laws.[29] Here the similarity ceased, for as a Whig and dissenting minister, Towers was far removed from some of Johnson's dearest principles.

At the outset of his *Essay,* Towers protested that his biography was to be an antidote to those lives already published. He assailed his predecessors, especially those of Johnson's friends who betrayed him by revealing his weaknesses or exaggerating his virtues (pp. 1–4). In this connection he charged that Mrs. Piozzi and Thomas Tyers were the chief violators who willfully ignored Johnson's flaws, and condescendingly excused their works on the grounds that little but panegyric was to be expected from Johnson's friends. Towers was sternly opposed to the apotheosis of Johnson and cast his lot, or so he said, with truth rather than decorum. Despite his recriminations, Towers did not hesitate to borrow liberally from other lives, as well as from Boswell's *Tour* and Johnson's works. He was especially derivative when dealing with the purely biographical aspects of Johnson's career. To the knowledge of Johnson's life he added virtually no fresh information.

Towers's account of Johnson's early years was valueless. He paid no attention to chronology (he relegated Johnson's birthdate to a footnote), moved rapidly over Johnson's career as a teacher, providing no picture of the frustrations Johnson suffered in that capacity, and neglected Johnson's Grub Street career.

Towers offered his *Essay* as a balanced, rational reply to earlier haphazard, biased accounts. He admitted from the start that his work was actually less a biography than a corrective treatise:

> It is not my design . . . to relate
> the transactions of his life, or to com-
> municate any new anecdotes of him:

but as so much has been written and
published concerning Dr. Johnson,
there may probably be some, who
may be desirous to form a rational
estimate of his character and of his
writings, who would judge impar-
tially of his excellencies and his defects; and it is with a view to con-
tribute in some degree to that end,
that this Essay is now offered to the
public (pp. 1–2).

To this announced purpose Towers was not always
faithful. To be sure, he balanced Johnson's power as
a writer against the strengths and weaknesses which,
he felt, were equally conspicuous in Johnson's character (pp. 2–3, 8). Although he spent little time on Johnson's personality apart from its influence on his writing, Towers conveyed the impression that he had carefully digested his thoughts. Where, for instance, some
biographers betrayed a sense of wonder that so great a
man as Johnson had imperfections, Towers was coldly
objective in his brief comments on Johnson's personality, particularly when he mentioned Johnson's intense struggles with indolence and melancholy. As he
said:

In Johnson, considered as a man,
and as a writer, there was much that
was excellent and laudable, and no

Drummond activ. pinx.

Engraved by Farn

DOCTOR JOSEPH TOWERS

> inconsiderable portion of what was
> otherwise. In forming our ideas of
> his character, we must separate the
> one from the other, if we would
> make a just and rational estimate
> (p. 5).

In the name of a "just and rational estimate" Towers took himself and Johnson much too seriously. He qualified his praise of the *Prayers and Meditations* as examples of true piety by remarking Johnson's poor attendance at public worship. Furthermore, he accused Johnson of blindness to his own greatest fault — "arrogance of behavior" — without providing examples of arrogant conduct (pp. 10–12). Much of his criticism was vitiated by his failure to perceive Johnson's sense of humor; he occasionally censured Johnson for inconsistent remarks to Mrs. Thrale, never realizing that some of them were uttered in jest or that Johnson enjoyed contradicting himself in the play of conversation. Here, of course, Towers's lack of acquaintance with his subject severely handicapped him. He repeated his charge of blatant inconsistency in his concluding sketch of Johnson, but without any attempt to probe Johnson's ostensible motives for it (pp. 107–8). He esteemed Johnson's charity towards Miss Williams, Mrs. Desmoulins, and Dr. Levett, but unwisely denied Mrs. Piozzi's claim that Johnson's zeal for truth was all-consuming (pp. 14–16).

Towers was usually careful to emphasize Mrs. Piozzi's most glaring hyperboles regarding Johnson's place in history, and ridiculed her upholding Johnson as a model Christian and then betraying her assertion by revealing Johnson's defects. He defended the notion of biographical discretion by protesting that as a friend, Mrs. Piozzi ought to have suppressed compromising anecdotes (pp. 19–20). By treating much of what she said too seriously, he was guilty of the very credulity of which he accused her. Had Towers recognized more fully Johnson's own awareness of his flaws and his unceasing struggle to master them, he might not have oversimplified the situation so drastically as he did.

On the surface, Towers's criticism of Johnson's works resembled Shaw's, although it was less detailed. Yet there existed fundamental differences between their estimates. Towers, for example, made no attempt at real biographical criticism, either through detailed examination of the works themselves or through efforts to relate them to particular periods of Johnson's life and thought.

Towers stood alone, however, in his recommendation of *all* of Johnson's poetry. Whereas a number of the other biographers expressed the wish that Johnson had written less poetry, Towers regretted that he had not written more. His admiration was somewhat qualified, however, because he focused entirely on Johnson's two great poems, offering little more than rudimentary criticism — he called attention to the "imperfect rhymes" of *London,* and questioned Johnson's motives in writing it, implying that had Johnson lived in more fortunate circumstances, he never would have composed the poem. Because he did not support such conclusions he left himself open to charges of hasty conjecture. The same was true of his comments on *Irene*. Towers bestowed approval on the play's observance of the unities and on its "elegant and nervous language" (pp. 29–30). As did almost everyone else, he objected to its declamatory quality and its coldness. But on the whole, he commended the play and mildly attacked the audience for neglecting its "general merit" (p. 30). And like Shaw, he strongly implied that *Irene* fell victim to poor taste and faulty staging.

Although high in his praise of Johnson as poet, Towers felt that the cornerstone of Johnson's literary reputation was the *Rambler*. He recognized that these essays were relatively unpopular when they first appeared, and like other biographers, he quoted from No. 208 Johnson's farewell address to the reader (pp. 32–33). In the main, his views on the *Rambler* were conventional, although at one point he called this production "delightful," a description used by no other biographer. Towers found especially commendable the "pure" morality, the "rational" piety, and the "acute and instructive" observations on life and manners (pp. 33–34). Here, of course, he penetrated the very heart of the *Rambler*'s virtues. Like "L" before him, he lauded the Eastern tales and the allegories,[30] and even compiled a small list of those *Rambler* and *Idler* essays he considered the best. In both cases, those papers he cited were the ones which treated of moral and philosophical considerations, an indication that Towers preferred Johnson's "heavier" writing.

Towers spent much less time with the *Idler* than with the *Rambler*. Although he differed from Shaw in protesting that the *Idler* essays were unequal to their predecessor, he lamented their having been neglected. He was unable — or unwilling — to recognize their light tone, for he seemed mystified that Johnson, as he informed Mrs. Piozzi, should have satirized himself in the character of Sober in *Idler* No. 31. Again, he showed his unnerving tendency to take Johnson too seriously, and also revealed that his lack of acquaintance with his subject led to rash statements.

In view of the contemporary appeal of the *Dictionary*, Towers's reticence in discussing this work is striking. His short description of Johnson's obscurity at the time he wrote the *Plan* in 1747 is valuable, and he applauded this piece for its elegance and its ample demonstration that Johnson was suited for the task (p. 27). However, the section on the *Dictionary* itself was surprisingly brief, partly because he underplayed the Johnson-Chesterfield quarrel, taking no cognizance of its importance as an illustration of Johnson's independence. Although he quoted from Johnson's description of the hardships under which he labored, Towers failed to analyze the passage in order to cast light on Johnson's achievement. Fully confident in the refinement of eighteenth-century language and diction, Towers reserved special approval for Johnson's establishment of a "common standard" by which the English tongue, he thought, was rendered permanent (pp. 38–39).

Towers's most effective criticism was that of *Rasselas*, which he misdated 1758. The chief virtue of this section was his brief analysis of the characterization in Johnson's novel. As far as we know, he was the only biographer to undertake character analysis of *Rasselas*. He praised the sustained representation of Imlac, approved his dissertation on poetry in the famous tenth chapter, and esteemed the character of the Arabian chief who captured Pekuah. All he found to quarrel with were the conversations between Rasselas and Nekayah, chiefly because the princess was nothing more than a philosophical mouthpiece for her creator.

Another interesting aspect of Towers's remarks on *Rasselas* was his brief observation on the gloom which he said pervaded the book and which he thought unwarranted "by truth or reason." He connected the dismal atmosphere of the novel with "those fears of some derangement of understanding, and that morbid melancholy, with which Johnson was not unfrequently afflicted" (p. 41). Although the connection he made between the dark reality of *Rasselas* and Johnson's melancholy was rather tenuous as he presented it, at least the possibility of such a relation existed in Towers's mind. That he mentioned it at all proved that he was aware, if only to a slight degree, of the relationship between the cast of Johnson's mind and his writing. That Towers failed to elaborate on this point may, in all likelihood, be attributed to his adherence to the demands of decorum.

In conjunction with most other biographers, Towers placed little value on Johnson's political pamphlets, not because he felt that Johnson descended from his hero's pedestal, but because he disagreed violently with Johnson's political principles. All Towers commended in the tracts was their style; as for the rest: "it would be injurious to the interests of truth, and to the common rights of human nature, to speak in terms of much commendation" (pp. 44–45). He called Johnson's position unconstitutional and "repugnant to the common rights of mankind," and accused Johnson of concealing illogical thought behind high-sounding but empty rhetoric (pp. 45–46). To Towers, Johnson's political writings were more subversive than Swift's. The only excuse he could discover for Johnson's malignance, one which he himself disbelieved even as he offered it, was that Johnson was trying to be humorous by deliberately exaggerating his views.

Towers's treatment of Johnson as political writer was one of the most vigorous of all contemporary attacks on Johnson's stature as a hero:

> However we may respect the memory of Johnson, and however unwilling we may be to speak of him with harshness, those who impartially peruse his political publications will be obliged to confess,

that few party pamphlets have appeared . . . which contain greater
malignity of representation (pp. 46–
47).

Still, a slight hint of hero-worship was evident in Towers's lament over Johnson's "indecent" sentiments in
Taxation No Tyranny (p. 49). The tone of this entire
section was a mixture of anger and condescension.
Towers reacted bitterly to Johnson's political stance,
yet "in apology for [Johnson], it may be admitted, that
he was a Tory from principle, and that much of what
he wrote was conformable to his real sentiments" (p.
50). Johnson, in other words, could not help being
what he was. Towers thus played a significant role in
constructing the popular myth of Johnson as an unremitting Tory, a myth which has only recently been
questioned.[31] On the whole, Towers's was a most un-
compromising attack on Johnson's political works. In
view of Towers's later attacks on some of Johnson's
Lives, the reasons for this attitude are not difficult to
assign.

It is Johnson as critic that interested Towers most.
Almost half the *Essay* covered Johnson's criticism,
throwing the biography far out of balance. Towers's
general opinion of the *Lives* was more adverse than
usual among Johnson's critics. He perceived a distinct
division between biography and criticism, and argued
that Johnson was adept only in the latter, a view which
some modern critics would endorse. Towers wrote that

as pure biography the *Lives* were exceptionable and factually undependable, but that as "compositions . . . abounding with strong and acute remarks, and with many very fine, and some even sublime passages," they possessed "unquestionably great merit" (p. 53).

Towers selected thirteen of the *Lives* for comment, including that of Edward Young written, as he noted, not by Johnson but by Herbert Croft.[32] To each of these biographies he devoted about a paragraph, usually dwelling upon one point he wished to make: for example, he praised the *Life of Butler* for its critical remarks without noting that it was one of the first English critical biographies; he charged Johnson with favoritism in the *Life of Dryden,* of bias and inaccuracy in the lives of Addison and Pope, of underestimating Prior's poetry, and of malignancy in the *Life of Swift.*

Towers's main concern was the *Life of Milton,* to which he devoted twenty-seven pages, or nearly one-fourth of the *Essay.* This long digression, a vindication of Milton's character, conduct, and, above all, his political notions, was the clearest example of biographical imprecision and imbalance in all of the early lives of Johnson. In defending Milton's memory, Towers misrepresented Johnson's position: "He could not endure those high sentiments of liberty, which Milton was so ardently desirous to propagate" (p. 56). Nothing more ridiculous could have been said about Johnson's attitude towards liberty, although it was true that he quarreled with many of Milton's objectives and methods. But Towers's rash assumption led him to commit inexcusable errors. He misapplied a quotation from Johnson regarding Milton's plea for the reformation of the universities (pp. 59–60); he rescued Milton from the same charge (inattention to public worship) he had earlier directed against Johnson (pp. 10, 77–80); and he accused Johnson of charging Milton with plagiarism of the *Ikon Basilike* when actually Johnson had merely repeated the charge made against Milton in his own lifetime (pp. 81–82).

Towers's disapproval of Johnson's attitude towards Milton's political views was symptomatic of his dislike of Johnson's own political opinions, expressed elsewhere when Towers criticized the lives of Waller and Henry King (pp. 54–56, 88–89), and in his concluding remarks, where he attacked Johnson's narrow conservatism (pp. 113–14).[33] It was obvious, therefore, that Towers's assault on Johnson's *Milton* was merely part of a broader disapproval of his political ideas.

Aside from his wrong-headed misrepresentation of Johnson's political views as they affected the *Life of Milton,* Towers's defense of Milton left Johnson more or less in the shadows. Taken from their context, Towers's remarks on Milton were clear, accurate, and well-reasoned; but in the midst of a biography of another man they were mere digressions. He laid undue stress on Milton's virtues to the point where Johnson, the ostensible subject of his *Essay,* nearly disappeared. He complicated matters, moreover, by introducing a long refutation of Thomas Warton's attack on Milton (pp.

70–77). This digression, together with those on Cowley, Hume, and the poetic justice of Archbishop Laud's unhappy death argued convincingly that Towers failed to maintain focus. Despite his protest of objectivity at the outset, Towers allowed his emotional attachment to Milton's ideals to overcome his "rational" plan, and his lack of control greatly impaired his work.

In justice to Towers, it must be said that he played fair with Johnson's criticism of Milton's poetry, although he slighted it, merely lauding Johnson for displaying the merits of *Paradise Lost* (p. 83). It was this fairness that caught Boswell's eye, for he commended Towers's biography as "very well written, making a proper allowance for the democratical bigotry of its authour; whom I cannot however but admire for his liberality in speaking . . . of my illustrious friend." [34]

Basically, Towers's objections to Johnson as a critic were balanced and judicious. Earlier in the *Essay*, he had bestowed qualified praise on the *Preface to Shakespeare*, and voiced the conventional disappointment in the edition itself (pp. 43–44). But near the end, he disputed Tyers's contention that Johnson was a born critic by citing as his chief defect his prejudice, couched as it was in forceful language and received with entirely too much unquestioning reverence by his friends (pp. 94–96). He chastised Johnson particularly for his dislike of blank verse and pastoral poetry, and aligned Johnson's antipathy to pastoral verse with his inability to appreciate natural scenery (p. 97).

Towers's criticism of Johnson as a biographer was

71

primarily adverse. Although he praised his style and insight into human affairs, he allied himself on the side of biographical decorum by stipulating that Johnson's greatest fault as a biographer was "too great a propensity to introduce injurious reflections against men of respectable character, and to state facts unfavourable to their memory, on slight and insufficient grounds" (p. 101). Although he professed deep concern for biographical truth, Towers obviously felt that breaches of discretion must be prevented; in cases where the truth was difficult to ascertain, he argued, "it is best to err on the favourable side" of the subject's character (p. 101). He also resorted to the notion of the moral practicality of biography by averring that "no benefit can be derived to the interests either of virtue, or of learning, by injurious representations of men eminent for genius and literature" (p. 101). This was precisely why he could praise Johnson's *Life of Savage,* even though it had been considered too favorable to the poet (pp. 25–26).

Towers closed his critical remarks on Johnson's writing with a brief examination of his style (pp. 114–17). His was a representative account of the contemporary reaction to Johnson's style. Towers defended Johnson, though not convincingly, against the most frequent charge against his style, its heavy-handedness and Latinate diction. He singled out for special commendation Johnson's use of words found in almost every earlier English writer, thereby refining and improving the language through his reworking of previous styles (pp. 115–16).

In the final analysis Towers's *Essay* was an apt illustration of prejudiced biography. The irony of his bias was, of course, heightened by his claim to rationality and impartiality at the beginning of his work when he attacked his predecessors for the very faults he was about to commit. And since this life appeared almost two years after Johnson's death, haste played no part in its imbalance and imprecision, not to mention its hostility. In attempting to reverse the tide of what he considered excessively partial biography of Johnson, Towers lapsed into unthinking criticism and, at times, sheer diatribe.

Of the four lives discussed, only two — Shaw's and Towers's — were biographies in any strict sense of the word. The accounts in the *Universal Magazine* and in the *European Magazine* were confessedly biographical material rather than genuine biography. By focusing almost entirely on Johnson as a writer, giving only occasional glimpses of him as a man, these writers necessarily limited their scope. But a limited range was their intention. To be sure, the occasional introduction of purely biographical elements and facts was usually abrupt and often incoherent, but for this they should be pardoned. One must remember that their resources were limited, and that they worked under the pressures of booksellers who demanded quick publication to take advantage of Johnson's still forceful reputation.

Because these biographers did not include dramatic accounts of Johnson's conversation and of the highlights of his career — because, in other words, they were not Boswells — modern critics have tended to ignore them or dismiss them as unworthy of attention. Yet it was not the purpose of these men to record dramatically the little incidents which revealed Johnson's character. They were interested mainly in his writings, the verbal expression of his knowledge, wisdom, and feelings. In this sense, they remained, for the most part, faithful to the preconceived concept of Johnson, although their own prejudices — for or against him — marred some of their work. Unfortunately, fidelity to one's image of his subject is not enough when only one portion of that subject's career is revealed and studied. These biographies, then, were only half-biographies in the sense that, owing to the strictures of biographical decorum, or to lack of information, or to a firm belief that the writer *is* the man, they portrayed only one side of Johnson's many-faceted personality. For a more complete account we must turn to those works which dealt with Johnson primarily as a moralist, a man who influenced other men through his own actions and conversation as well as through his writings.

CHAPTER THREE

JOHNSON THE MORALIST

As we have seen, some of the early biographers of Johnson conceived of him as essentially a writer, and projected their image of him largely in terms of his literary accomplishments. Other biographers, while applauding his literary genius, saw Johnson primarily as a man whose works were subsidiary to his character (though, as they realized, his character was eminently present in his writings) and whose fame rested principally upon the moral tenor of his life. He deserved commemoration because he was considered as perhaps the most powerful moral influence of his age.

The early lives to be discussed in this chapter took a different approach to Johnson. It was natural that in their concentration on Johnson as a writer such biographers as Shaw and Towers ignored or suppressed much purely biographical data — anecdotes, letters — which had come their way. But the biographies which portrayed Johnson as a moralist and emphasized his character were scarcely more intimate than those which attended mainly to his writings. This lack of intimacy can be attributed in part to the pressures of decorum. In the long run these biographers (Thomas Tyers excepted) did not reveal much more about Johnson's character, conversation, private moments, and social relationships than those treated earlier. These biographers, visualizing Johnson as a moral hero, were confronted directly with the question of suppressing unpleasant information which showed that many of Johnson's personal qualities were not in keeping with the desired image of a national moral hero. The picture of Johnson the man was sometimes painful; the spectacle of Johnson the moralist (which often discounted the man) was edifying, and these biographers felt it their duty to present the latter.

Johnson's death provoked widespread literary reaction. In the year which followed, countless epitaphs, elegies, and odes appeared in the newspapers and journals, most of them written by persons who had never known him and who sought to capitalize on his passing to initiate or further their literary careers. These pieces, though crudely written, were a reliable index to the immediate effect of Johnson's death. And almost without fail, they apotheosized him as a saint whose death, in the words of Thomas Hobhouse, "shall teach the world to live." [1]

I

To Thomas Tyers (1726–1787) went the honor of writing the first "animated" biography of Johnson, *A Biographical Sketch of Dr. Samuel Johnson.*[2] Next to the account by Mrs. Piozzi, Tyers's was the most charming and informal biography written before Boswell. And if one judges from Boswell's reminiscences of Tyers, the reason for such charm was not far to seek.[3] Tyers was the son of the proprietor of Vauxhall Gardens and he himself held a share in the spa until 1786. Doubtless Boswell, in describing him as ill-bred to the law because of his "handsome fortune, vivacity of temper, and eccentricity of mind," felt a sense of kinship with Tyers.[4] Boswell's description of Tyers as a man who "ran about the world with a pleasant carelessness, amusing everybody by his desultory conversation," though reasonably accurate, has stigmatized Tyers as a sort of harmless playboy.[5] And this image was further enforced by Johnson's modeling "Tom Restless," the would-be critic of *Idler* No. 48, after Tyers.[6] Yet Tyers endeared himself to Johnson, for as Boswell noted, he lived with Johnson "in as easy a manner as almost any of his very numerous acquaintance," and this was no small feat.[7]

Because Tyers was a dilettante author who printed only a few copies of his writings, the publishing history

77

of the *Sketch* is somewhat muddled. It was first published in the *Gentleman's Magazine* in December 1784, with addenda following in the Supplement and in the number for February 1785. It was also reprinted at least three times in 1785.[8] Tyers was, nevertheless, a careful writer whose *Political Conferences between several Great Men in the last and present Century* (1780), a series of dialogues, won Boswell's admiration for its learning and discrimination of character, two assets necessary for any biographer.[9] John Wilson Croker interpolated large segments of the *Sketch* into his edition of Boswell, and testified to Tyers's accuracy (which Boswell had challenged) and to the fact that all other biographers borrowed from Tyers in one way or another. Boswell, despite his fondness for Tyers, accused him of being "among the various persons ambitious of appending their name to that of my illustrious friend," and underrated the *Sketch* as an "entertaining little collection of fragments." [10]

Actually the appeal of the *Sketch* was effected almost in spite of itself. Tyers's basic principle of organization was not chronological, but was loosely topical, a seemingly undisciplined, unpatterned presentation of segments of Johnson's career. He flitted about, butterfly-like, conveying the impression of spontaneity. His statement of purpose was a masterpiece of sprezzatura: "What he knows and can recollect, he will perform" (p. 4). At times such posturing led Tyers to neglect his duty, as when he failed to divulge the identity of Johnson's benefactor at Oxford, saying he "may

THOMAS TYERS

be known to enquiry" (p. 4). Similarly, near his conclusion, Tyers inserted with a casual mention of his forgetfulness some information that, for the sake of coherence, should have been used earlier (p. 24).

Even when Tyers apologized, recognizing the disadvantages of hasty composition, he did so in relaxed fashion: the "hurry" of his pen prevented his tracing Johnson's early writings (p. 5); he warned the reader that this was only a sketch which "looks forward and backwards at the same time" or that his work "hits imperfect accents here and there" (p. 13). But the very casualness of such apologies constituted a charm in itself and contributed in no small measure to one of the chief appeals of the *Sketch* — its relaxed honesty.

Unlike most of the other biographies of Johnson, Tyers's life owed much of its effect to its style. His style was as far removed from the Johnsonese sometimes affected by other biographers as it was possible to be. His stylistic ancestor, in fact, was John Aubrey, whose shorthand sentences Tyers imitated successfully. Tyers's was a winning style, informal and conversational, calculated to draw the reader into the writer's fond and easy reminiscences of a man whom he knew, admired, and loved.

Tyers was a master at packing insight into a quick turn of phrase, as when he justified Johnson's voracious appetite by saying that it operated only after "he had subdued his enemy by famine" (p. 2), or when he joined Johnson's amazement at Isaac Newton's lifelong celibacy by asserting that "curiosity . . . might have led him to have overcome that inexperience" (p. 14). His use of homely similes was apt. He explained, for instance, that Johnson, like many prodigies, by-passed childhood for "early ripeness, just as the Russian winter turns into summer without passing through spring," likened Johnson's precocity to "Hercules in his cradle" (p. 4), and compared his indolence to "Columbus at the oar" (p. 13). Often he indulged in deliberate euphuism: "But perhaps Johnson had more of life by his intenseness of living" (p. 2); "He was willing to endure positive pain for possible pleasure" (pp. 2–3); "He wrote to live, and luckily for mankind lived a great many years to write" (p. 7). In these examples Tyers strove for stylistic effect less for its own sake than in the service of character delineation. Although such phrases are arresting, their main purpose was to provide an Aubrey-like epigrammatic description of Johnson's personality and career. Moreover, Tyers was adept in the use of quotations from Johnson's talk to embellish his portrait; for example, in describing Johnson's poor eyesight he quoted Johnson's now-familiar remark that he "had not seen out of that little scoundrel for a great many years" (p. 5).

This charm, however, was disarming. It concealed Tyers's full awareness of what he was about, and over-emphasis on charm alone often obscures his self-consciousness and makes his achievement little more than a stylistic *tour de force*. Although his relaxed posture and light style contributed much to the general charm of the *Sketch*, the piece had its serious moments.

For one thing, Tyers, unobtrusively but unmistakenly, insisted on his own authority for many of the stories he related. At the end of the *Sketch* he reported that Johnson, noticing how Tyers eyed him closely, once predicted that Tyers "at some time or other . . . might be called upon to assist a posthumous account of him" (p. 24). Another example of Tyers's concern to establish his own authority was his careful noting that he himself had heard Johnson express amazement at the success of the *Rambler,* and in view of Johnson's conclusion in *Rambler* No. 208 as well as other accounts of the ill-success of these essays, Tyers's testimony was important in establishing the authenticity of his comment (p. 9).

Elsewhere, too, Tyers was cautious. He protested that he had the permission of Dr. James Dunbar to reprint excerpts from Johnson's derisive remarks on Hume (p. 19), and asserted that he had proof that it was Robert Dodsley who first suggested to Johnson the idea of undertaking the *Dictionary* (p. 7). In dealing with some of the more controversial moments in Johnson's life Tyers exercised prudence. He refused to dwell on the Johnson-Macpherson debate, and carefully protested that he held nothing against Chesterfield although he described fully his quarrel with Johnson. In order to clarify this matter, he attempted to secure a copy of Johnson's letter to the Earl for inclusion in the *Sketch,* but his applications (including one to Bennet Langton) failed (pp. 7–10). Furthermore, Tyers was aware of the prevailing notion of decorum, and although his account was intimate and revealed many of Johnson's foibles, Tyers at least paid lip service to the demands of discretion by exclaiming that Johnson's correspondence would never be published because "the world will never be trusted" (p. 15).[11] Also, he obeyed the rules of discretion when he admitted that he had not provided any other "compiler" with anecdotes of Johnson (p. 25). He even apologized with needless scrupulosity for including so many quotations from Johnson's conversation; actually excerpts from Johnson's talk were not prevalent in the *Sketch*.

Thus, for all his delightful impressionistic technique, Tyers recognized his duties as a biographer. He was neither as desultory and careless as he pretended to be nor as Boswell and Birkbeck Hill estimated him to be.

Tyers commenced his biography in somewhat brave fashion by applying to Johnson Charles II's remark that Cowley, after his death, "had not left a better man behind him in England," and then going on to reverse the usual procedure by beginning not with Johnson's birth but with his death (pp. 1–2). Towers, as we have seen, inveighed against this so-called misrepresentation, but Tyers no doubt succeeded in grasping the reader's attention with this device. It was obvious from the outset that Tyers's aim in the *Sketch*, despite its panegyric start, was not to extol Johnson as a hero, but to portray him as he knew him — as a man whose personal and moral worth triumphed over his flaws. Throughout the *Sketch* Tyers did not hesitate to call attention to Johnson's cantankerous behavior. Tyers was on the defensive, and a perceptible pattern in his work was his continuous effort to defend Johnson from aspersion without ignoring or suppressing the very qualities that made him a man rather than a bloodless hero. Although weakened somewhat by his failure to explore Johnson's motives fully, Tyers's defense was forceful in its refusal to neglect or play down the compromising features of Johnson's life and personality. Johnson, for him, was a man to be touched, not a hero to be admired from afar lest his blemishes be discovered. His account of Johnson's career at Oxford, for example, stressed Johnson's surly conduct, but without sensationalizing it. Only by considering Johnson as a man, implied Tyers, could he be made an imitable moral example.

Tyers's method of portraying Johnson as a moralist, then, was to reveal him as a person. Tyers organized the *Sketch* around the presentation of anecdotes gleaned primarily from his own observation and from Johnson's other friends. He had the knack of using his personal knowledge of Johnson's habits to make both heavy and light touches in his defense without intruding his own presence as Boswell and Mrs. Piozzi so often did. One example of his seriousness was his attempt to show that Johnson's eating and drinking habits, however open to malicious over-emphasis, were in fact moderate and that his occasional abstinence was closely connected with those religious sentiments which made his life a preparation for death (p. 2). He also made the point that Johnson's was a thoroughly Christian death even if colored by fear, and that the miserable conditions under which he had passed part of his life were a source of Johnson's courage in his final days. Tyers reverted to light touches to heighten the effect of Johnson's appearance, as when he confessed that he always looked away during Johnson's occasional fits of paroxysm, or that Johnson's speech in later years was hampered by "dental losses" (pp. 3, 22). He could smile, too, at Johnson's supposed credulity regarding the Cock Lane ghost. These light strokes, without detracting from Tyers's devotion to Johnson, neatly balanced the heavier moments of his interpretation, and enforced his conception of Johnson as a moral hero who was also human.

A further aspect of Johnson's life which Tyers sought to clarify was his political creed. Like most other biographers, Tyers admitted that Johnson was a Tory, but unlike them, he qualified his statements by disclosing Johnson's flexibility in matters political and his desire to avoid political bickering. "He was content," wrote Tyers, "to let his enemies feed upon him as long as they could" (p. 12). He defended Johnson's acceptance of the pension by claiming that his action illustrated his ability to argue against the cause in which he believed so as to test his companions and to sharpen his argumentative powers. Similarly, he was not surprised by the rapport between Johnson and Wilkes at

Dilly's famous dinner, shrugging it off as merely another illustration that Johnson "did not write his animosities in marble" (p. 21). He also presented a balanced account of Johnson's attitude to Scotland, even though he regretted Johnson's lack of propriety in speaking of that country. Tyers, however, excused Johnson on the specious grounds that John Cleveland's poems on Scotland were more "malignant" than anything Johnson ever wrote or said against it (p. 10).

Of greater import was Tyers's endeavor to correct the impression of Johnson as an unremitting pessimist, a notion which he considered an affront to Johnson's character. To combat this misconception, he warned against the hasty attribution of perpetual gravity and despair to Johnson's thought. "Who," he asked, "can determine of the pleasure and pain of others," and this was a pertinent question seldom asked by Johnson's biographers (p. 14). What was thought to be rank pessimism was instead shrewd common sense applied to the general existence of mankind as Johnson apprehended it. As Tyers put it:

> Johnson thought he had no right
> to complain of his lot in life, or of
> having been disappointed: the world
> had not used him ill; it had not
> broken its word with him; it had
> promised him nothing; he aspired to
> no elevation; he had fallen from no
> height (p. 14).

Tyers offered, in addition, a valuable study of Johnson's conviction that human happiness and "natural and moral good" prevailed over evil in human affairs (pp. 13–14). According to Tyers, Johnson manifested his firm belief in this proposition in conversation, and in his unceasing charity to friends and strangers alike (pp. 15, 19). The most remarkable element of Tyers's presentation, colored at times by his personal recollection of Johnson's charitable acts, was the absence of sentimentality or undue emphasis.

Tyers protested that the *Sketch* was not a "record office" for Johnson's sayings (p. 21), but printed many of them anyway, some for the first time.[12] Near the conclusion, in fact, he fired many of Johnson's witticisms in machine-gun fashion, but normally he integrated them into the text with skill. His, as a matter of fact, was one of the first English biographies to make some attempt to demonstrate the importance of conversation as an indication of a man's character.

Because he was Johnson's close friend, Tyers's comments should be weighed carefully, especially in light of the paucity of remarks by other biographers on Johnson's conversation. Tyers was careful not to exaggerate Johnson's versatility and genius in conversation lest his picture lose its desired effect. Nevertheless, a few of Tyers's remarks on Johnson's talk were among the most widely circulated by his contemporaries. Johnson himself, alluding to his reticence in starting conversation, admitted that Tyers had described him best with his remark, "Sir, you are like a ghost: you never speak till you are spoken to." [13] He wittily summed up Johnson's notion of conversation and its moral effect when he said that Johnson "always talked as if he was talking upon oath" (p. 16), and that "if he wrote for money, he talked for reputation" (p. 17). Apart from Mrs. Piozzi, Tyers was the only biographer who mentioned that Johnson was an adept manager of conversation, often steering it to topics favored by other members of the group in order to glean information from them (p. 16). Similarly, he was the first biographer to describe Johnson's reluctance to divulge his sentiments to those who eagerly sought his judgment of their writings or of another book. In order to correct the legend of Johnson as a rude conversationalist who wantonly brandished his weapons, he stressed Johnson's desire not to create enemies or alienate friends (pp. 6, 23).[14]

For Tyers, Johnson the man was of greater interest than Johnson the writer, for his moral genius was more forcefully displayed in person than on paper, and since Tyers knew Johnson well, he sought to share his experience with the reader. As he said, Johnson's conversation "was thought to be equal to his correct writings" (p. 17). He entertained great respect for Johnson's learning, but to his mind Johnson's intellectual prowess was inseparable from his moral strength. Tyers never wearied of describing Johnson's wide-ranging curiosity — "A spark was enough to illuminate him" (p. 22). In this connection, Tyers, alone among the early biographers, indicated Johnson's close acquaintance with Greek, Roman, and continental literature (pp. 15–16). His general estimate of Johnson's achievements in learning was further heightened by the knowledge that throughout much of his life Johnson pursued knowledge with extraordinary vigor in the face of poverty and ill health. This last point will be of even greater significance when we come to William Cooke.

If, as Tyers admitted, Johnson was the "great lay-preacher of morality to the nation" (p. 9), he was so chiefly through the example of his life, less so through his writings. Tyers, however, was not blind to the value of tracing Johnson's literary career. "There is here neither room nor leisure to ascertain the progress of his publications," Tyers wrote, "though it would exhibit the history of his mind and thoughts" (p. 7). Tyers, whether he realized it or not, did in fact "exhibit the history of his mind and thoughts," but with only scant attention to his writings and virtually no critical or psychological analysis. Nevertheless, as Greene has disclosed, Tyers contributed to the identification of the canon, adding works to the 1785 pamphlet that he had not included in his original article.[15] But as a systematic discussion of Johnson's literary career, the *Sketch* was worthless. Tyers's most extended discussion (and it was brief) was that of Johnson as a critic, for which post, Tyers argued, "he was fitted by nature" (p. 19). His most perceptive remarks were made on the *Lives* which, he said, provided the "pulp without the husks," related personal histories with skill, and were superlative examples of literary criticism (p. 19). His most acute remark, still echoed by modern critics in defense of Johnson's critical independence, was that the foundation of Johnson's taste was his knowledge of human nature rather than the study of other critics. Incisive glimpses such as this indicate that Tyers would have been a perceptive critic of Johnson's work had he so chosen. But he did not so choose, and his comments on other works were merely scattered at random throughout the *Sketch*.

That Johnson was a moral example mattered for Tyers; what mattered even more was *how* Johnson was a moral example. And this point was crucial to Tyers's interpretation. If, as he protested, "Johnson had more of life by his intenseness of living" (p. 2), this very intensity lay at the core of effectiveness as a moral instrument and of his appeal as a man. Unfortunately, Tyers left undeveloped his presentation of Johnson's restless pursuit of knowledge, but his tantalizing account threw out enough hints to make the reader recognize that without his intense desire to experience life in all its variety and complexity, Johnson's high moral stature would probably never have existed, much less have been proclaimed. Tyers's greatest appreciation for Johnson was devoted to his "surveying life in all its modes and forms, and in all climates" by which he attained his "great knowledge in the science of human nature" (p. 17). This intensity, Tyers admitted, had its dangers: "his imagination often appeared to be too mighty for the controul of reason" (p. 3), but this was a disadvantage over which Johnson ultimately triumphed and for which he was a more effective moralist. It was regrettable that Tyers, who was apparently well-informed of Johnson's social life, did not see fit to explore his social relationships. He considered briefly and sympathetically Johnson's relationship with the Thrales, and bestowed kind words for the considerate treatment the brewer and his wife gave to Johnson (he suppressed all reference to her second marriage), but this was the only instance of this type of concern. He preferred to ruminate in his inimitable way on Johnson's active morality rather than to dramatize it at length.

For Tyers, Johnson's whole life was a moral testament. His respect and love for Johnson shines through every page of the *Sketch* without being maudlin. Because he did not give a systematic account of Johnson's life, his estimate of Johnson is perhaps difficult to assess. It is clear, however, that Tyers considered Johnson's victory over life's hardships and disappointments, his hard-won literary and social eminence, as a sort of pilgrim's progress which could inspire all Christians.

II

In marked contrast to the casualness of Tyers's biography was the grave tone of *The Life of Samuel Johnson, LL.D.*, written by William Cooke (d. 1824) and published anonymously by George Kearsley within two weeks after Johnson's death.[16] Cooke, often called "Conversation Cooke" after the title of one of his poems, was professor of Greek at Cambridge. He wrote biographies of Samuel Foote and Charles Macklin, and published recollections of Goldsmith in the *European Magazine* (1793).[17]

Cooke was also a minor figure in the Johnson circle and a member of the Essex Head Club; his discussion of this group in the *Life* was disappointingly brief although he did indicate that the meetings were Johnson's main escape from melancholy. He probably edited Kearsley's anthology, *The Beauties of Johnson,* first published in November 1781, and very popular until the mid-nineteenth century.[18] Although personally acquainted with Johnson, Cooke made little effective use of his acquaintance in the *Life.*

Cooke was the first biographer to borrow Johnson's scheme of organization in the *Lives of the Poets.* The biography proper occupied the first section. It was developed chronologically with much attention given to Johnson's works and to high points of his life. A concluding character sketch considered Johnson under such headings as philologist, theologian, historian, and poet. Unlike Johnson, Cooke was more concerned with his subject's life than his works. In addition, he was the first biographer to reprint a copy of Johnson's will (copies had been printed in newspapers and periodicals), to publish Johnson's efforts on behalf of the ill-fated Dr. Dodd, and to offer a catalogue of Johnson's writings.[19] Cooke's *Life,* therefore, was the most comprehensive biography to appear before Hawkins's in 1787.

Prefixed to the biography was a brief Advertisement propounding Cooke's notion of biography and betraying his short-sighted attitude towards selectivity of detail. He refused, for example, to discuss Johnson's early writings because he felt they lacked sufficient variety and consequence to mark any progress in his literary development. He confined these productions to the catalog of works at the end of the *Life*. Cooke was also vigorously opposed to the accumulation of details, and attempted to forestall criticism of his work in this manner:

> Some critics may perhaps object, that in so long and distinguished a life as that of Dr. Johnson, I have not . . . followed him from *house to house,* and *lodging to lodging,* or introduced the first copies of his most celebrated works, with all their *original blots* and *interlineations.* — To more curious inquirers I consign this task, my purpose being *only* to give a *sketch, warm from the life* — by which the general character of the man, and of his writings, may be known (pp. iii–iv).[20]

He repeated this argument against the relevance of trivia in the text itself, mentioning the difficulty and unimportance of such a scrupulous attention to the dates of Johnson's writings (p. 21), and protesting that he could print neither the entire *Plan of the Dictionary* nor fragments thereof, lest the whole work be destroyed (p. 25). Much of this argument, however, was really a shield for his obvious haste in writing the *Life,* a haste which occasionally led Cooke to violate his own dictum by introducing irrelevant details and anecdotes which interrupted or obscured his narrative.[21]

To his credit, Cooke made his concept of Johnson clear from the start, a concept which, for the most part, he developed consistently. He followed the conventional idea of biographical utility. But, to his mind, Johnson transcended the usual role of the biographical hero because he united *"integrity* and *great abilities"* to become a subject not only for instruction but for admiration as well (p. 1). Cooke therefore established a double significance for Johnson as an example to all men: "a man whose writings entitle him to the first rank in the classes of literature — his morals, to the first classes among men" (p. 2). Later he called Johnson "as proud a name as any of them in *literature* — a greater than most of them in *morals"* (p. 86). At times this theory led Cooke to oversimplify matters, as when he explained the rise of Johnson's literary reputation in terms of his moral character, which "always went hand in hand" with his fame as a writer (p. 21). It was obvious that Cooke's sole preoccupation was to present Johnson as a moral figure — almost as a hero — and this attitude accounted partly for the relative neglect of Johnson's writings *qua* literature. It also led him to confine Johnson's formative years to a few paragraphs,

WILLIAM COOKE

for in Cooke's view Johnson's early life contributed little to his stature as a moral example. Cooke quickly brought Johnson to London, where, as he ironically observed, his talents "would be sooner and more accurately discovered" and "sooner and more liberally rewarded" (p. 5).

The dominant theme of Cooke's *Life* was Johnson's moral heroism. In his honest and valuable portrait of Johnson's physical appearance and habits, Cooke described Johnson as being of *"heroic stature"* (p. 82).[22] Like some of the biographers already discussed, Cooke thought that Johnson was destined to live in London where he could achieve greatness, and he was grateful for the lost appointment to the mastership of the grammar school near Lichfield because Johnson "would have missed the opportunities of calling out his great and various abilities" (p. 14). Cooke was careful, in describing this nearly-divine intervention in Johnson's behalf, to color the highlights of Johnson's life in such a way that the overtones of heroism would be readily apparent without necessarily obviating the fact that Johnson was also a human being. In this case, Cooke took note of Johnson's keen disappointment at the failure of his application for the mastership and his subsequent loss of a leisurely occupation while at the same time he stressed the fortunate outcome of this "disappointment" of Johnson's hopes. Although the Johnson of Cooke's *Life* was not quite the flesh-and-blood individual of Tyers's *Sketch*, neither was he a pale example of abstract moral virtues.

Cooke embellished his accounts of Johnson's quarrels with Tom Osborne and Chesterfield by making something of a martial hero of Johnson as he defied those who sought to oppress him in his work (pp. 18–19, 26–29). Similarly, Cooke saw Johnson locked in a perpetual struggle against the avarice and machinations of the booksellers, with the implication that his writings were worth much more than he ever received because they were written in the service of truth (pp. 30, 87–88). In this connection he was careful to defend Johnson against any charges of avarice, particularly in his dealings with the booksellers (pp. 62, 79–80). Johnson's demand for an additional five hundred pounds for the *Dictionary,* he argued, was a necessity because "the work could not possibly be finished without it; the author having no pecuniary source to apply to." It was also justified in terms of the time and labor expended on the task (p. 30). He then explained how Johnson came to die worth two thousand pounds and attributed the accumulation of this sum to Johnson's frugality in living and his prudence in preparing for old age (p. 87).

But Cooke treated the moral tenor of Johnson's life in other ways, too. His account of Johnson's relations with Tetty, though brief, was designed to show that Johnson's motives for marrying her were sincere and that he remained a tender husband until her death (pp. 12, 36–37). Yet his description was so brief that it was necessarily oversimplified.[23] To prove that Johnson was a devoted son, Cooke reprinted in its entirety

Idler No. 41, presented as written in memory of his mother. To Cooke, Johnson's sentiments in this essay demonstrated that he was not only a good son but a fervent Christian. Furthermore, Cooke wished to make clear the circumstances of the paper so that its meaning would be more easily understood. But he missed the whole point; namely, that the essay showed Johnson's active morality, his ability to feel profound grief without losing his perception of the underlying reasons for it, the lesson to be gained from it, and the need to respond in an emotional yet rational manner.

Another way in which Cooke fostered the image of Johnson the moralist was to draw him as a "most severe and unremitting student" (p. 83), in contrast to Tyers's representation, which had revealed Johnson's rather haphazard reading habits. Cooke placed little stress on Johnson as an active moralist who mingled with London society on all levels. Rather, he preferred to show Johnson's total involvement with teaching, translating, and writing almost to the exclusion of living in the world (p. 83). His inaccuracy is all the more surprising since he knew Johnson personally. Why Cooke chose to underplay this aspect of Johnson's career is a mystery, unless he was deliberately suppressing information which he thought might have detracted from Johnson's stature.[24]

But it was in his picture of Johnson's final days that Cooke was most concerned to paint Johnson in the colors of a firm Christian moralist. His account, comparatively speaking, was a detailed one, and he, like many others, saw Johnson's as a model Christian death. Cooke used quotations which displayed Johnson's firm faith, his refusal to bow to pain and the knowledge of impending death, his efforts to retain his intellectual power (expressed in his note to William Allen after the paralytic stroke of 1783) — all were related with an appeal for emulation. Unfortunately, Cooke's reverence for Johnson's moral courage took the form of an eighteenth-century equivalent of a modern "sick" joke when, reporting the results of the autopsy performed on Johnson, he wrote that Johnson's "heart was *uncommonly large,* as if analogous to the extent and *liberality of his mind"* (p. 76). He also called attention to Johnson's Christian generosity to his servant, Francis Barber, as evidence of his moral virtue (pp. 77–78). Despite his inclusion of some of the unpleasant details (such as the autopsy findings and the destruction of Johnson's papers), Cooke's description of Johnson's last days was a crucial part of his effort to defend Johnson's stature as a moral example whose death was a model for all Christians.

The spirit of Johnson's moral heroism also crept into Cooke's treatment of Johnson's writings. He devoted considerable space to Johnson's literary career, but much of what he said was intended less as literary criticism than as a revelation of Johnson as a moral writer whose productions promoted the cause of truth (p. 14). In this light, he asserted that *London* and *The Vanity of Human Wishes* must be read with delight and improvement, but he never explored their poetic technique or effect (p. 11). The *Life of Savage* he exalted as an "elegant and moral performance," but he accused Johnson, quite incorrectly, of softening some of Savage's weaknesses out of friendship. Although he recognized Johnson's ability to picture the "novelty and vicissitudes of a man of expedience," it was evident that Johnson's biography appealed to Cooke in terms strictly moral (pp. 19–20).

The heroic qualities of Johnson's literary career, Cooke thought, were best displayed in his reaction to the failure of *Irene* and the drudgery of the *Dictionary*. Cooke described Johnson's sheer persistence in his work on the *Dictionary* as a Herculean effort: "He conceived the design of one of the noblest and most useful, though at the same time the most laborious work that could possibly be undertaken by one man" (p. 25). But Cooke merely repeated here what almost everyone else felt, and so he did not deal with this topic at length. Cooke was grateful for the failure of *Irene,* because it discouraged Johnson from writing other plays and forced him to seek "more substantial honours" in the *Rambler* and the *Dictionary* (pp. 24–25). Although it led him to demean the status of the tragedian, Cooke was aware of Johnson's psychological reaction to the collapse of his play. Like Hawkins (who dwelled persistently on Johnson's moral courage), Cooke saw the failure as a spur to Johnson's imagination and to his quest for literary success. "Foiled in his first attempt," proclaimed Cooke, "he was determined to rise, like

Antaeus, from his fall; and put in claims for higher and more substantial honours" (p. 25).

Two works which Cooke praised in unreserved moral terms were the *Rambler* and *Rasselas*. He called *Rasselas,* for moral reasons, a "beautiful little novel" (pp. 49–50). Unlike most eighteenth-century observers, Cooke placed the *Rambler* on equal footing with the *Tatler* and the *Spectator,* a brave boast grounded largely on the force and energy with which it disseminated philosophic and moral truth (pp. 31–32).[25] Cooke made one incisive observation, later seconded by Arthur Murphy, that the Latinate diction of the *Rambler* was influenced heavily by Johnson's work on the *Dictionary*.[26]

Since Cooke felt that "the principal merit" of the *Rambler* consisted in "disseminating philosophic and moral truths with peculiar force and energy," he considered the *Idler* an inferior performance and compared it to "the last impressions of a good print, in which the likeness remains, though the strength is considerably diminished" (p. 43). His effort to accentuate Johnson's moral achievement in literature led him, at times, to overscrupulous concern for the gravity of Johnson's moral themes and pronouncements. This narrow-mindedness illustrates how undue attention to the image of the biographical subject can result in the distortion of the subject's abilities.[27]

As was to be expected, Cooke was also solicitous of Johnson's political reputation. He regretted the publication of the political pamphlets, arguing that Johnson unthinkingly exposed himself to charges of hypocrisy and support of ministerial corruption. Up to a point, Cooke acceded to the belief that Johnson's unduly acrimonious treatment of the opposition had damaged his reputation, but he only half-heartedly and unconvincingly defended him with the argument that if politically wrong, Johnson must be credited with thinking his views were right (p. 54). No defense would have been better than this.

Cooke's bias for the morality of Johnson's works did not dominate his remarks throughout the *Life*. At times he was capable of disinterested scholarship, although none of it was extensive. For example, he provided one of the few contemporary accounts of the arrangement by which the *Parliamentary Debates* were published, and knowledge of the factors of composition certainly added further proof of Johnson's skill in individualizing characters. Cooke, too, was one of the few men to commend the taste and judgment of Johnson's account of the Harleian Library, and to mention Johnson's authorship of the Prologue to Goldsmith's *The Good Natured Man* and of Goldsmith's epitaph. He was honest as well. He valued *Irene* for its "Eastern magnificence," its "fine sentiments and elegant language," but admitted that Johnson was not a good stage dramatist (pp. 23–24). Cooke, like Towers and the writer for the *European Magazine,* esteemed Johnson's poetry, lamenting that he had not written more (pp. 89–90). His esteem of the *Lives* as greater criticism than biography was conventional, although he praised

Johnson's concentration on the small moments of men's lives rather than the notorious ones, thereby contradicting his own sentiments expressed at the outset of the *Life*.

We do not intend to convey the impression that Cooke's portrait of Johnson was distorted by excessive worship. Although less concerned with Johnson's foibles and failings than Tyers, Mrs. Piozzi, or Boswell, Cooke sometimes dented his subject's armor. He was, for example, the only biographer to relate the anecdote (and he did so in the dramatic Boswellian manner) of Johnson's being momentarily taken aback in his intent to write a *Dictionary of Trade and Commerce*. Johnson, as Cooke mentioned, was riding the crest of fame after the appearance of the *Dictionary* and, "perhaps buoyed up a little too much with this opinion" that "his name was a tower of strength to any publication," proposed to a group of booksellers that he undertake a *Dictionary of Trade and Commerce*. "This proposal," Cooke wrote, "went round the room without his receiving any answer, at length a well-known *son of the trade,* since dead, remarkable *for the abruptness of his manners,* replied, 'Why Doctor, what the D——l do you know of trade and commerce?' The Doctor very modestly answered, 'Not much, Sir, I confess in the *practical* line — but I believe I could glean, from different authors of authority on the subject, such materials as would answer the purpose very well' " (p. 34). Likewise, he mildly censured the harshness of Johnson's attack on Macpherson (pp. 56–57), and later quoted passages from the lives of Milton and Congreve which pained him (pp. 60–62). More important, he maintained that great as it was, Johnson's knowledge was not universal. He did not make extravagant claims for Johnson's learning, but he offered the wrong reasons for its limitations by saying that Johnson's heart "was too unsuspicious of the world, to resist, at all times, the infinite variety of its impositions" (pp. 90–91). He then cited Johnson's credulity in the case of the ghost at Cock Lane as an example of Johnson's lack of practical knowledge of the world, failing to recognize Johnson's intense desire to explore all aspects of human experience in order to ascertain truth and satisfy his restless curiosity.

Though less lively than Tyers's account, Cooke's report of Johnson's conversation was one of the strengths of his biography. Obeying the strictures of decorum, Cooke pointed out in the first edition that he could have included many examples of Johnson's wise sayings and *bon mots,* but he denied that biography was the "proper place" for such insertions (p. 101). Although in the second edition he succumbed somewhat to popular taste and observed that some specimens would be "no improper *appendage* to these memoirs" (p. 91), he did not change his basic position.[28] The chief virtue of Johnson's talk, to Cooke's mind, was its didacticism as the "great variety of his reading broke in upon his mind, like mountain floods, which he poured out upon his audience in all the fullness of information" (p. 91). Consequently, Cooke paid little attention to the manner of Johnson's conversation, merely pointing out its economy and Johnson's over-zealous defense of the field against all opposition. What counted mainly for Cooke was the vast power of memory which Johnson displayed in conversation, and he related at length two anecdotes in which Johnson revealed his astonishing memory. The first anecdote was Johnson's quoting in Latin from the Tenth Satire to prove the justice of Juvenal's description of the infirmities of old age (pp. 92–95). The second, and more remarkable, instance, concerned John Hawkesworth's *Ode on Life*. Hawkesworth visited a friend's home to polish the poem and while there he met Johnson.

> . . . as Hawkesworth and the Doctor lived upon the most intimate terms, the former read it to him for his opinion, 'Why, Sir,' says Johnson, 'I can't well determine on a first hearing, read it again, second thoughts are best;' Dr. Hawkesworth complied, after which Dr. Johnson read it himself, approved of it very highly, and returned it.
>
> Next morning at breakfast, the subject of the poem being renewed, Dr. Johnson, after again expressing his approbation of it, said he had but

one objection to make to it, which was, that he doubted its *originality*. Hawkesworth, alarmed at this, challenged him to the proof; when the Doctor repeated *the whole of the poem,* with only the omission of a very few lines; 'What do you say now, Hawkey,' says the Doctor? 'Only this,' replied the other, 'that I shall never repeat any thing I write before you again, for you have a memory that would convict any author of plagiarism in any court of literature in the world' (pp. 96–97).

The account of this scene, especially in Hawkesworth's reaction to Johnson's playful gibe, rivals many of the scenes in Boswell, Mrs. Piozzi, and Fanny Burney's diary. These were the two most extended dramatic sketches in the entire *Life*. Objectively speaking, Cooke's description of Johnson's conversation was too brief to be satisfactory; considered in the context of some of the other lives, however, it was worthwhile. It is well to compare Cooke's appreciation with that of Tyers to see two different effects produced by Johnson's talk. Cooke valued its moral instruction and said virtually nothing about its vigor and animation; Tyers appreciated it above all for its manner, though he did not ignore its moral effect. Tyers, too, indicated that Johnson was often humorous and witty in his sallies, whereas Cooke, who was evidently blind to Johnson's quick and witty humor, said nothing of this quality.

But Cooke's most heartfelt admiration for Johnson was based on the fact that he was *"an honest man* and *good Christian,"* and these were the "noblest parts of his character" (p. 98). Here, near the conclusion, Cooke made his most conscientious if rigid attempt to humanize Johnson, but did so within a firm moral framework. For Cooke, the two primary virtues of Johnson's character were his refusal to pander to the folly and vice of the age and his use of literature as a forum from which to advance the cause of virtue and truth. Cooke admired Johnson's total commitment to the theory that literature was a viable and effective means by which to better the world (he quoted at length Johnson's warning to vicious authors in *Rambler* No. 77), but unfortunately his admiration led him to make an oversimplified coupling of Johnson the man with Johnson the writer — the exact reverse of the modern outlook on Johnson. "His life," commented Cooke, "reflected the purity and integrity of his writings" (p. 100).

Since he knew Johnson late in life, he must have been aware of the powerful melancholy which afflicted Johnson (knowledge of his malady was widespread even among those who did not know him), and must have suppressed this information. Also, his picture of the nature of Johnson's friendships conveyed the false notion that Johnson was on good terms with almost everyone, and this obviously was not the case. In addition, Cooke sought to prove that in Johnson the disciplines of learning and Christianity were indissolubly united. Cooke's posture in this matter was less defensive than Tyers's, but he carefully noted that despite Johnson's great learning, he was always pious and punctual in the practice of Christian duties. As the *Prayers and Meditations* were to demonstrate later, such was not always the case.

III

Some eighteenth-century lives were more significant for what they said about biography than they were as biographies, and they showed that in many cases biographical criticism ran well ahead of biographical practice. A cogent illustration of this fact was the sixteen-page *The Life of Samuel Johnson, LL.D.* prefixed to the Jarvis edition of the *Dictionary* published in 1786.[29] Nearly worthless as biography, it was significant for its strident defense of biographical decorum. This life was largely derivative and was given over to a chronological listing of Johnson's writings, interspersed with a few commonplace anecdotes, but its importance lay in the first two pages, wherein the question of decorum was discussed.

This biographer, like Cooke, thought Johnson was trapped in the scholar's ivory tower, but he was more vocal than Cooke on this point. Johnson's, he wrote, was a "life marked only by the common sterility of inactive literature," a life "still, quiet, eventless" (pp. 1, 2). He later contradicted this assertion when, after re-

counting the story of Johnson's vain attempt to obtain
the mastership of the school in Appleby, he remarked
that Johnson "was again thrown amongst all the shoals,
storms and difficulties of a life of professional literature" (p. 8). Although he was the only biographer to
define Johnson as a "professional" his prevailing —
and misguided — attitude was that Johnson was a
cloistered figure who never swam in the high tide of
humanity.

More than any other early biographer of Johnson,
he valued a man's right to personal privacy. He as-
saulted the previous biographers for having irreparably
damaged Johnson's reputation through the "ill-di-
rected zeal of injudicious friendship" manifested in
the folly of this "new and base species of intellectual
anatomy" (p. 1). He protested that these lives dealt
severe blows both to the dead and the living. Not
only was Johnson's posthumous reputation contam-
inated, but the names of persons still living (he identified none) were damaged because the biographers,
in recalling Johnson's conversation, made him dis-
avow friendships once considered secure. He dedicated
his brief sketch to those sensitive souls who, like him,
felt a "ready and animated abhorrence of a conduct
that tends at once to give instability, to every humane
opinion, and to diffuse uncertainty and suspicion
through every human attachment" (p. 1).

Using this argument of the far-reaching social and
moral consequences of biographical misconduct, this
writer scored Johnson's *Life of Savage* on the same

basis as he attacked the lives of Johnson, namely, that Johnson injured Savage's reputation by betraying his irregularities (pp. 8–9). He also introduced the specious argument that the *Life of Savage* betrayed the inefficacy of Johnson's moral influence in steering Savage from his dissolute life.[30] But again he was inconsistent in his opinion. He attacked the candor with which Boswell had described Johnson's attitude towards the Highlanders, yet castigated Boswell for having shown the journal entries to Johnson, thereby destroying the possibility of impartiality and sincerity (p. 12). He accused Boswell of sheer flattery and of concealing Johnson's real sentiments. This was a curious reversal of his field, for at the outset, as we have seen, he had defended panegyric.

Generally speaking, he was unhappy about one aspect of a biographer's duty which, in the late eighteenth century, was just gaining general recognition; that is, the penetration into the subject's mind and soul, his thoughts and feelings, in order to trace his intellectual and moral development and to explore the nuances of his actions, writings, and personal relationships. But this writer argued that such probing not only injured the moral and literary character of the subject, but also destroyed his "comfort" (p. 1). In other words, he attacked this "new" form of biography on both public and private grounds. The result of such inquiry, he maintained, was that all public figures would virtually surrender their privacy for fear of being perpetually spied upon. Nothing would be left, he

continued, except purely artificial behavior, both public and private. He obviously overstated his case, but
so did many other supporters of biographical propriety.
This writer further undermined his own position by
arguing that circumspection was an indispensable in-
gredient in biography (p. 2). Obviously, then, he supported the conventional theory that biography should
be a largely commemorative work designed to uphold
and foster the prevailing image of a famous man.

In this light, the next step in his argument was the
depreciation of trivia. Like Cooke, he claimed that "it
is with the view of the human character as with all
other prospects, too many circumstances confound;
they destroy what critics call integrity or wholeness"
(p. 2). Thus, it was foolish and irresponsible to include
a hundred specimens of a man's wit when ten would
do. But he failed to realize that specimens by themselves would not do, that the context in which they
were uttered often colored the effects of conversational
interplay. Unfortunately, this writer merely desired
to show the existence of certain qualities and abilities
in a man; he did not recognize that their mere existence
did little to humanize him, that with disciplined, skill-
ful selection and arrangement these details could make
a man not merely an example, but a living example.

Perhaps one of the reasons why he was so adamantly
opposed to the use of details had to do with the loca-
tion of his biography. As a mere preface to the *Dictionary*, the *Life* could not be extensively detailed —
he called this a species of "negative merit." It is worth

noting, too, that despite his attack on details, he did not hesitate to use them himself, especially some of the unpleasant ones concerning the manner of Johnson's dying, although he employed them with his purpose clearly in mind of delineating Johnson's "general character." He provided reasonably detailed accounts of Johnson's friendship with Savage, of his altercation with Osborne (much of which he borrowed from Tyers), of the circumstances surrounding the composition of *Rasselas* (although he failed to explain why these were as important as he said they were), and of Johnson's final months, where he included snippets of Johnson's conversation (again borrowed from Tyers).

Moreover, despite his animadversions against the earlier biographies, he borrowed extensively from Cooke, Mrs. Piozzi and his primary target, Boswell. About a fourth of his essay was made up of word-for-word transpositions from the *Tour* and the *Anecdotes,* from the latter of which he appropriated the brief description of Johnson's youth. In so brief a biography, the unoriginal and perfunctory manner in which he performed his duties was astonishing.

One of the greatest flaws in this biography, owing partly to spatial limitations, was its imbalance, seen primarily in excessive quotation from such early works as "Anacreon's Dove," "On a Lady's presenting a Sprig of Myrtle to a Gentleman," and "Ad Urbanum," and the corresponding neglect of quotation from, and reference to, more substantial works. Indeed, together with the letters of Walmesley and Gower, Johnson's letter to the Lord Chancellor and his note to Allen after his paralytic stroke in 1783, quotation constituted a large part of the *Life,* a further indication of the writer's indolence and his refusal to seek out fresh knowledge about his subject. Even at the end, when he discussed Johnson in paragraphs devoted to his career as scholar, critic, poet, essayist, lexicographer, and narrator, he merely repeated conventional estimates and contributed no critical insights whatever. Perhaps his whole attitude was best declared when he said that "with the account of his literary history must pretty well terminate the relation of every thing that can be important or interesting in a life like his" (p. 12). With such an attitude, by no means unique in eighteenth-century theory where a man's life and writings were thought to be facilely separable, little indeed could be expected from this biographer.

It cannot be doubted that to his generation Johnson was a moral hero. The biographies discussed here represented a more or less general response to Johnson. They proved that no small portion of his fame — as man, teacher, and writer — was derived from his moral stature. And it was Johnson's courage, his intense desire not merely to hold his fears at bay but to conquer them as well, which endeared Johnson to such people as Tyers. Johnson's unquenchable thirst for experience, perhaps his most appealing quality to the modern student, appealed as forcefully to his contemporaries. Even in these comparatively incomplete lives, we can observe that the biographers had some awareness, however limited and general, of Johnson's refusal to compromise with the problems of human existence. To be sure, none of them presented a systematic analysis of Johnson's moral vision, although they took some halting steps in this direction. But how systematic, one may ask, was Boswell's account of Johnson's moral views? Not very. But his contemporaries were aware, as the Archdeacon of Hayley's *Two Dialogues* showed, that Johnson's "perilous balance" was an integral component of his moral nature, that he was engaged in a perpetual, often painful, balancing of contrary forces in his own nature. True, Johnson's agonized wrestling with melancholy was occasionally misconstrued by these biographers, especially those who wished to make him a flawless moral hero. This short-sightedness, which can be explained partly as the consequence of adherence to the rules of biographical decorum, was the chief flaw in these biographies, apart from their incompleteness and incoherence. Johnson's negative spirit profoundly disturbed some of these biographers, who failed to perceive that his gloom was an unaffected index to the moral indignation inspired by what he often saw in life.

In projecting the image of Johnson as a moral hero, some of these writers vastly oversimplified certain aspects of his career, but the fact that such a vision of Johnson existed — and still exists — indicates some measure of perception by these biographers whose flaws and virtues alike contributed to the study of biography.

CHAPTER FOUR

"NO SPECIES OF
WRITING SEEMS MORE
WORTHY OF CULTIVATION
THAN BIOGRAPHY"

I will venture to say that [Johnson] will be seen in this work more completely than any man who has ever yet lived." But it was not Boswell alone who preserved him; his contemporaries probably realized this fact better than we. The flurry of anecdotes, epitaphs and elegies, memoirs, reflections, and formal biographies which appeared between 1784 and 1791 indicate that Boswell was neither the sole reporter nor the sole creator of Johnson's greatness. Ultimately, Johnson's greatness and his appeal transcend definition, a point amply demonstrated by the numerous attempts — contemporary and modern — to define it.

One way to study both Johnson and Boswell is to

examine the other biographies published before Boswell's. His biography, to be sure, far surpasses, but does not annihilate, his rivals. Although he supposedly gave us Johnson "warts and all," Boswell did not, through design and lack of information, paint the whole picture. His zeal for truth notwithstanding, Boswell did conceal painful and disturbing facts about Johnson's life, and reacted violently in print when Hawkins and Mrs. Piozzi disclosed them in their works.

The originality of such biographers as Tyers and Shaw has gone largely unnoticed. Most critics who are introduced to Johnson through Boswell are likely to forget that some of the anecdotes now familiar in his biography gained wide currency in the late eighteenth century in the biographies of his competitors.[1] In most instances, their original contributions to Johnson's canon and introductions of his letters and remarks are ignored.

The flaws of these early biographies are, of course, numerous. They were often poorly written and organized, and none of them pretended to completeness. If nothing else, they revealed the scarcity of information about Johnson's life which prevailed in their day. They introduced factual errors and compounded others. Clearly, these biographers fell victim to poor research and faulty evaluation of evidence. In some cases (Towers, for example), the biographers marred their work by undue prejudice against certain of Johnson's principles. Whether such lapses can be attributed to incompetence, haste, or the desire to pander to popular demand for biographies of famous figures is hard to determine. Perhaps all that can be said is that as biography some of these lives are decidedly marginal.

Nevertheless, the significance of these early biographies, we think, outweighs their defects. Their importance rests chiefly upon the following: their revelations about Johnson's contemporary reputation; their illustration of various attitudes towards Johnson; their complementing Boswell; and their role, however small it might appear, in the development of English biography. These biographies, if they accomplished little else, demonstrated the widespread public interest in literature in general and biography in particular. That they were sometimes hastily written and published did not preclude their illuminating pertinent biographical issues of the day. In this sense, the collective value of these biographies and anecdotal materials may count for more than the individual merits of each.

Few of the biographies can be called "creative" in the sense of artistic originality, yet only two of them (the essays in the *Universal* and *European* magazines) were mere recitations of facts. But even these two brief articles were invaluable in identifying many of Johnson's works for the first time. The lives all had their staple ingredients, usually borrowed from one another: eulogies, letters, certain anecdotes (Pope's response to *London,* Johnson's altercations with Chesterfield and Osborne, the Ossian affair), and lists of birth, death, and publication dates. Despite these similarities, each biography was in its own way different from the others.

Each biography was colored and limited (or, in the case of Tyers, enhanced) by the preferences and prejudices of the biographer towards biography in general and Johnson in particular. Each projected his own image of Johnson, but collectively they conveyed the two main images of Johnson as writer and moralist.

One further observation on these images is perhaps necessary. If the early biographies can be taken as representing general opinion of Johnson, then it would seem that his so-called dictatorship was perhaps moral rather than literary. Contemporary criticism of his writings was not by any means timid or submissive. If his literary reputation was a bit uncertain, his moral throne, at least, rested upon secure ground. The furor inspired by the early lives centered upon Johnson the moralist rather than Johnson the writer. It was only when Johnson's personal, not his literary, faults were disclosed that the early biographers came under fire.

As with many notable figures, Johnson's public and private lives were, in most respects, readily distinguishable. Those who, in the late eighteenth century, wished to make a moral hero of Johnson demanded strict attention to his public life alone. The relationship between a writer's intimate life and his work was often deemed an improper sphere for biography. The crucial point, of course, was the doubt cast on acceptable works of art by the awareness of the artist's personal imperfections. This, as we have seen, muddied the waters considerably with respect to Johnson. If the eighteenth century seemed greatly — even excessively — alarmed by the disparity between an artist's life and work, and consequently constructed stern moral requirements for the biographer, then what is one to think of the modern age when, as Lionel Trilling observes:

> How peculiarly modern a preference it is to emphasize the disjunction between the life and the work, to find an especial value in a 'perfect' work that arises from an 'imperfect' life.[2]

The eighteenth century, on the contrary, would have found it difficult to believe that a man's art can justify his life and that his life should not be allowed to detract from his artistic achievement. This is perhaps one of the primary reasons why, in the early lives, there are virtually no extensive attempts to probe Johnson's character. Mrs. Piozzi scattered "dark hints" throughout the *Anecdotes,* but Hawkins and Boswell were the first to explore at length the nature of Johnson's personality. For those whose appreciation of biography depends chiefly on its psychological penetration and presentation these early lives will undoubtedly be failures, for they deal with Johnson's character primarily in general terms.

To the modern reader Johnson is not less great because of the candor of his biographers; rather, he is greater and more sympathetic because we feel that his struggles with melancholy and illness make him a heroic figure and at the same time a man. The eighteenth-century reader, in contrast, found it nearly impossible to reconcile heroism with humanity. If contemporary critics reviled the impertinent curiosity of writers such as Boswell, Hawkins, Tyers, Towers, Cooke, Shaw, and Mrs. Piozzi, we, with the benefit of hindsight, can honestly say that it was the critics' loss. The great contribution of Boswell and Johnson's other biographers is not their labors on the canon, nor their introduction of new facts about his life, but their preservation and reconstruction of the life, full of incomparable conversation, wit, and wisdom, of Samuel Johnson.

APPENDIX A

i R., W. [William Rider]. "Mr. Johnson." *An Historical and Critical Account of the Lives and Writings of the Living Authors of Great-Britain. Wherein their respective Merits are discussed with Candour and Impartiality.* London, 1762. Pp. 7–10.

ii [Baker, David Erskine]. "Mr. Samuel Johnson, M.A." *The Companion to the Play-House: or, An Historical Account of all the Dramatic Writers (and their Works) that have appeared in Great Britain and Ireland, from the Commencement of our Theatrical Exhibitions down to the Present Year 1764.* London, 1764. 2: S6ᵛ–T1ᵛ; "Irene." 1: K6ᵛ. (See V, below.)

iii [Tytler, James?] "An Account of the Life, and Writings of Dr. Samuel Johnson." *Gentleman and Lady's Weekly Magazine* [Edinburgh], 28 January 1774, pp. 1–3.

iv "An Impartial Account of the Life, Character, Genius, and Writings, of Dr. Samuel Johnson." *Westminster Magazine* 2 (September 1774): 443–46.

v [Reed, Isaac, ed.]. "Samuel Johnson." *Biographia Dramatica, or, A Companion to the Playhouse.* London, 1782. 1: 256–58; "Irene." 2: 172. (A revised edition of II; see Appendix B.)

vi [Cooke, William?]. "Memoirs of the Life and Writings of Dr. Samuel Johnson." *The Beauties of Johnson.* 5th ed. London, 1782. Pt. 2, pp. vii–xv.

vii L. "Memoirs of the Life and Writings of Dr. Samuel Johnson." *Universal Magazine* 75 (August 1784): 89–97. Reprinted in *London Chronicle,* December 14–16, 1784, pp. 577–78; December 16–18, pp. 585–86; *Lloyd's Evening Post,* December 13–15, 1784, p. 569; December 15–17, p. 575; December 17–20, p. 581; December 20–22, p. 591; *The Craftsman; or Say's Weekly Journal,* December 18, 25, 1784; *Scots Magazine* 46 (December 1784): 609–12; Appendix, 683–87; *Town and Country Magazine* 16 (December 1784): 619–23; Supplement, 707–10; *Boston Magazine* 2 (May 1785): 172–76; (June 1785): 209–12; (July 1785): 249–51.

viii "An Account of the Writings of Dr. Samuel Johnson, including Incidents of his Life." *European Magazine* 6 (December 1784): 411–13; 7 (January 1785): 9–12; (February 1785): 81–84; (March 1785): 190–92; (April 1785): 249–50.

ix T. T. [Thomas Tyers]. "A Biographical Sketch of Dr. Samuel Johnson." *Gentleman's Magazine* 54 (December 1784): 899–911; Supplement: 982; "Additions." 55 (February 1785): 85–87. Issued with revisions as a pamphlet, *A Biographical Sketch of Dr. Samuel Johnson,* London, 1785. Reprinted in the *London*

Magazine Enlarged and Improved 4 (May 1785): 331–
48 (Taken from December *GM*); *New Annual Regis-
ter . . . For the Year 1784* 1 (London, 1785): 23–47
(Taken from pamphlet).

x   [Cooke, William]. *The Life of Samuel Johnson,
LL.D. with Occasional Remarks on His Writings, an
Authentic Copy of His Will, and a Catalogue of His
Works. To Which are Added, Some Papers Written by
Dr. Johnson, in Behalf of a Late Unfortunate Charac-
ter, Never Before Published.* London, 1785.

xi   [Shaw, William]. *Memoirs of the Life and Writings of the Late Dr. Samuel Johnson; Containing Many
valuable Original Letters, and several Interesting
Anecdotes both of his Literary and Social Connections.
The Whole Authenticated by Living Evidence.* London, 1785.

xii   Boswell, James. *A Journal of a Tour to the Hebrides, with Samuel Johnson, LL.D.* London, 1785.

xiii   [Towers, Joseph]. *An Essay on the Life, Character, and Writings of Dr. Samuel Johnson.* London,
1786.

xiv   Piozzi, Hester Lynch (Mrs. Thrale). *Anecdotes
of the Late Samuel Johnson, LL.D., during the last
twenty years of his life.* London, 1786.

xv "The Life of Samuel Johnson, LL.D." In Johnson, *A Dictionary of the English Language*. London:
Printed and Sold by John Jarvis, 1786. (16 unnumbered pages at the beginning of Volume 1.)

xvi Hawkins, Sir John. *The Life of Samuel Johnson,
LL.D.* London, 1787.

xvii [Harrison, James?]. "The Life of Dr. Samuel
Johnson." In Johnson, *A Dictionary of the English
Language*. London: Harrison and Co., 1786. (18 un-
numbered pages at the beginning of the volume.)

xviii Boswell, James. *The Life of Samuel Johnson,
LL.D.* London, 1791.

The tone and content for many of the later sketches seems to have been set as early as 1762 with the appearance of a 650-word panegyric in William Rider's *An Historical and Critical Account of the Lives and Writings of the Living Authors of Great-Britain*.[1] After mentioning Johnson's studies at Oxford and his keeping a private academy in Lichfield, the author observed that Johnson came to London and distinguished himself as a writer because he was by nature endowed with a genius to instruct mankind, and not teach boys. He felt that the *Rambler* would be sufficient to immortalize his name and it was compared favorably to the *Spectator*. The *Idler* was allowed to be superior to other essay writers of the day but not equal to the *Rambler*. Johnson's genius was praised as being "as various as prolific; he does not derive his Reputation as an Author from one Species of Composition" (p. 8). *Irene* was commended for its poetry, *Rasselas* and the "oriental Compositions" were lauded, and the *Life of Savage* was called a masterpiece. The sketch concluded with a paragraph extolling Johnson's moral worth:

> Not contented with surpassing other Men in Genius, he makes it his Study to surpass them in Virtue, and all that Humanity and that sin-

cere Attachment to Religion, which shine thro' his Writings, are equally conspicuous in his Life. Though by no Means in Affluence, he is always ready to assist the indigent; and being of a truly philosophical Disposition, he is satisfied with a Competency, tho' by the Superiority of his Talents, he might have long since made a Fortune (p. 10).

The next sketch, indebted for a number of its points to the previous account, was the most important to appear before 1784. It was first included in David Erskine Baker's *The Companion to the Play-House* (1764) and later revised and expanded for inclusion in Isaac Reed's edition of this work, *Biographia Dramatica, or, A Companion to the Playhouse* (1782). This account, in both its versions, influenced every biographical sketch of Johnson through the "Memoirs" in the *Universal Magazine*.

"An Account of the Life and Writings of Dr. Samuel Johnson," for example, which appeared in the *Gentleman and Lady's Weekly Magazine* for Friday, 28 January 1774, was taken almost entirely from the *Companion*, adding only that Johnson came to London with Garrick and routine praise of several of his prologues, political pamphlets and the Preface to his edition of Shakespeare, as well as brief mention of the forthcoming account of the tour through Scotland.

DAVID ERSKINE BAKER

Also in the *Westminster Magazine* for September 1774 appeared "An Impartial Account of the Life, Character, Genius, and Writings, of Dr. Samuel Johnson" which was largely an embellishment of the account in the *Companion* with a partial repetition of the "Short Character of Dr. Johnson" which appeared in the *London Magazine* for March 1773.[2] To this was added the "respectable Hottentot" sketch and a few anecdotes. Several paragraphs were devoted to the tour of Scotland, and Johnson is censured for his political pamphlets.

Finally, there was the "Memoirs of the Life and Writings of Dr. Samuel Johnson" which were published in the fifth edition of the *Beauties of Johnson* (1782). Approximately two-thirds of this was taken with only minor changes from the *Biographia Dramatica*.[3] The sketch was filled out with information taken from Thomas Davies's *Memoirs of the Life of David Garrick* and the well-known letter from the Earl of Gower to a friend of Swift's in an abortive attempt to get Johnson a Master's degree.[4]

Since this sketch, which first appeared in the *Companion* and later in the *Biographia Dramatica,* was so influential on the later lives, and because it seems to be representative of the public knowledge of Johnson (apart from occasional anecdotes) before 1784, it is reprinted below. The text is taken from the *Biographia Dramatica* and the material added in 1782 is enclosed in brackets. The only major revision in the text is recorded in a note.

JOHNSON, SAMUEL. This excellent writer, who is no less the glory of the present age and nation than he will be the admiration of all succeeding ones, [was the son of a bookseller at Litchfield, in the county of Warwick (sic). He was entered of Pembroke College, Oxford, on the 31st of October, 1728, but left the University without taking any degree. On his return to his native county, he appears to have devoted his attention to the education of youth; and Mr. Davies, in his *Life of Garrick,* p. 7, fixes the beginning of the year 1735 as the period when he undertook, as a private tutor, to instruct Mr. Garrick and some other youths in the *Belles Lettres.* This mode of instruction, however, could not have lasted long; for, in the succeeding year, 1736, we find him advertising to board and teach young gentlemen in general the Latin and Greek languages at Edial near Litchfield. Yet his last scheme perhaps not answering his expectation, he left the country in March 1737, and, what will be thought remarkable, in company with Mr. Garrick, who at the same time first launched into active life. At London again our author appears to have met with disappointments which disgusted him with the town; for in August 1737, we find him desirous of returning again into his native county to take upon himself the office of master of a charity-school in his neighbourhood then vacant, the salary of which was sixty pounds a year. But the statutes of the school requiring the person who should be elected to be a master of arts, this attempt seems to have been frustrated.] [5] Having conceived the design of one of the noblest and most useful, though at the same time the most laborious works that could be possibly undertaken, viz. a compleat Grammar and Dictionary of our hitherto unsettled language; he drew up a plan of the said design, in a letter to the right honorable the earl of Chesterfield, which being published, gave the strongest proof, in its own composition, how great a degree of grammatical perfection and classical elegance the English tongue was capable of being brought to. The execution of this plan cost him the labour of many years; but the manner in which it was at last executed made ample amends for all the expectations of the public in regard to it for so long a time; and the honours paid him on the occasion of its publication by several of the foreign academies, particularly by the Academia della Crusca, leave all encomium on the work in this place entirely superfluous. During some intervals of recess, necessary to the fatigue of this stupendous undertaking, Mr. Johnson published many other pieces, which are most truly capital in their kind; among which the *Rambler,* a series of periodical essays, which came out twice a week for two years successively, stood in the foremost rank. In the course of so great a number of these papers as this long period demanded, those which the undertaker of them was favoured with by others, was inconsiderable; and yet, on the whole, the product of this single genius, thus perpetually employed, proved at least equal, if not superior, to that of the club of first-rate wits, who were concerned in those celebrated works the *Spectator* and *Tatler*. Dr. Johnson's stile in prose is nervous and classically correct; in verse his numbers are harmonious and musical, yet bold and poignant, and, on the whole, approach nearer to Mr. Pope's manner of versification than that of any other writer; and though he has favoured the world with but little in absolute verse (for all his Prose is Poetry), yet that little, like diamonds of the first water, will ever be held in the highest estimation, whilst gems of larger bulk, with less intrinsic worth, are scarcely looked upon. [When Mr. Pope had read his *London,* and received no satisfactory answer to repeated enquiries concerning its author, his observation was, "It cannot be long before my curiosity will be gratified; the writer of this poem will soon be *deterré.*"] In short, while the name of Juvenal shall be remembered, this gentleman's improved imitations of him, in his two satires, entitled *London,* and *The Vanity of Human Wishes,* must be read with delight. His imagination is amazingly extensive, and his knowledge of men and manners unbounded, as may be plainly traced in his Eastern stories in the *Rambler,* in which he has not only supported to the utmost the sublimity of the Eastern manner of expression, but even greatly excelled any of the oriental writers in the fertility of his invention, the conduct of his plots, and the justice and strength of his sentiments. His capital work of that kind, however, is a novel, entitled *Rasselas, Prince of Abyssinia,* too well known and universally read to need any comment here, and in which, as he does at present, so he probably ever will, stand without an equal.

[Our author indeed was formed to sustain the character of an exalted moralist; and never was known to descend from himself till he became a political writer. When talents designed for the support of religion and truth are prostituted to the defence of royal and ministerial errors, who is not ready to exclaim with Pistol — *Then did the sun on dunghill shine!*]

Dr. Johnson has written only one

dramatic piece, the success of which was not equal to its merit, owing entirely to his having too strictly adhered to the Aristotelian rules of the drama to render his piece agreeable to the taste of our present theatrical audiences, who look for little more than plot and incident, without paying any great regard either to character, language, or sentiment; it was performed at Drury-Lane Theatre, and is entitled,

Irene. Trag. 8vo. 1749.

It would, however, be the highest injustice, after bestowing these undeniable encomiums on his genius, were I not to observe, that nothing but that genius can possibly exceed the extent of his erudition, and it would be adding a greater injury to his still more valuable qualities, were we to stop here, since, together with the ablest Head, he seems possessed of the very best Heart at present existing. Every line, every sentiment, that issues from his pen, tends to the great centre of all his views, the promotion of virtue, religion, and humanity; nor are his actions less pointed towards the same great end. Benevolence, charity, and piety, are the most striking features in his character; and while his writings point out to us what a good man ought to be, his own conduct sets us an example of what he is.

[His last undertaking, *The Lives of the Poets,* would alone have been sufficient to immortalize his name among his countrymen. The excellence of this work is powerful enough to extinguish even the indignation which his political tenets (so frequently incorporated with his critical remarks) may sometimes have excited in those of an opposite way of thinking.

Within a few years past, the Universities of Oxford and Dublin have presented him with the honorary degrees of master of arts, and doctor of laws, as their testimonials of his public merits. May it be long before he seeks the place which only can supply a reward adequate to his private virtues!]

IRENE. Trag. by Samuel Johnson. Acted at Drury-Lane, 8vo. 1749. This is the only dramatic piece among all the writings of this celebrated author. It is founded on the same story with the foregoing; the author, however, has taken some trifling liberties with the history, *Irene* being here made to be strangled by order of the emperor, instead of dying by her own hand. The unities of time, place, and action are most rigidly kept up, the whole coming within the time of the performance, and the scene, which is a garden of the Seraglio, remaining unmoved through the whole play. The language of it is, like all the rest of Dr. Johnson's writings, nervous, sentimental, and poetical. Yet, notwithstanding these perfections, assisted by the united powers of Mr. Garrick, Mr. Barry, Mrs. Pritchard, and Mrs. Cibber, all together in one play, it did not meet with the success it merited, and might therefore justly have expected.

CUE TITLES

Davis — Bertram H. Davis, *Johnson Before Boswell: A Study of Sir John Hawkins' LIFE OF SAMUEL JOHNSON* (New Haven, 1960).

Greene — Donald J. Greene, "The Development of the Johnson Canon," *Restoration and Eighteenth-Century Literature,* ed. Carroll Camden (Chicago, 1963), pp. 407–22.

Hazen — Allen T. Hazen, "The *Beauties of Johnson,*" *Modern Philology* 35 (February 1938): 289–95.

Johnsonian Miscellanies — *Johnsonian Miscellanies,* ed. G. B. Hill, 2 vols. (Oxford, 1897).

Letters — *The Letters of Samuel Johnson,* ed. R. W. Chapman, 3 vols. (Oxford, 1952).

Life — *Boswell's Life of Johnson,* ed. G. B. Hill, revised and enlarged by L. F. Powell, 6 vols. (Oxford, 1934–1950); vols. 5 and 6, 2nd ed., 1964.

Nichols, *Anecdotes* — John Nichols, *Literary Anecdotes of the Eighteenth Century,* 9 vols. (London, 1813–1815).

Nichols, *Illustrations* — John Nichols, *Illustrations of the Literary History of the Eighteenth Century,* 8 vols. (London, 1817–1858).

Waingrow — *The Correspondence and other Papers of James Boswell Relating to the Making of the LIFE OF JOHNSON,* ed. Marshall Waingrow (New York, 1969).

NOTES

PREFACE

1   The quotation from Tyers is from his *Sketch,* p. 14
(see Appendix A); *Gentleman's Magazine* 54 (December 1784): 883–84; William Gerard Hamilton's observation appears in the *Life,* 4: 420–21; Murphy: "His
death kept the public mind in agitation beyond all
former example," *Essay on Johnson's Life and Genius,
Johnsonian Miscellanies,* 1: 356; More: "His death
made a kind of era in literature," William Roberts,
*Memoirs of the Life and Correspondence of Mrs. Han-
nah More,* 2nd ed. (London, 1834), 1: 394. Lort's
letter to Percy appears in Nichols, *Illustrations,* 7: 467–
68; Boswell's in *Letters of James Boswell,* ed. C. B.
Tinker (Oxford, 1924), 2: 336. The letter is dated
12 July 1786. Boswell, in a letter to Anna Seward of
11 April 1788, mentioned the "luxuriant freshness" of
Johnson's fame (*Letters,* 2: 348). An exception to the
general sentiment concerning Johnson's Christian
death was voiced by Anthony Pasquin: "The tremu-
lous manner in which Doctor Johnson died has, in
my idea, been more detrimental to the general interests of Christianity, than any other event appertaining
to a single individual." See *Eccentricities* of John Ed-
win (London, 1791), 1: 328.

1 For an informative recent discussion of this problem, see James L. Clifford, "How Much Should a Biographer Tell? Some Eighteenth-Century Views," *Essays in Eighteenth-Century Biography,* ed. Philip B. Daghlian (Bloomington, Ind., 1968), pp. 67–95.

2 Lucyle Werkmeister, *Jemmie Boswell and the London Daily Press, 1785–1795* (New York, 1963), p. 12. See also Clifford, "How Much Should a Biographer Tell?"

3 For the last item, see *Gentleman's Magazine* 55 (June 1785): 412.

4 The unknown author of *More Last Words of Dr. Johnson* (1787), a pamphlet which, according to the title page, was composed by "Francis, Barber" was doubtless an attempt to capitalize on the notoriety of the lives written by Johnson's acquaintances. This pamphlet, described in the *European Magazine* 12 (December 1787): 466–67, as an "impudent and most abominable imposition on the public," still stands as the epitome of vulgar exploitation of Johnson's fame. In it, Johnson's reputation and intellectual excellence are analyzed from an examination of his feces. The work also included many coarse anecdotes, all of them manifestly untrue. Needless to say, Johnson's servant, Francis Barber, did not write the pamphlet.

5 In another notice in its issue for 14–17 January 1785, the *London Packet* transferred some guilt to

Johnson: "The friends of Dr. Johnson seem not to be tired of debasing his memory. The anecdotes they have given, if they prove anything at all, prove an insufferable brutality and vanity to have been the leading features in His character. . . ."

6 *Life,* 4: 423.

7 Rev. William Field, *Memoirs of the Life, Writings and Opinions of the Revd. Samuel Parr, LL.D.* (London 1828), 1: 164–65.

8 Ibid.

9 Parr, according to his most recent biographer, planned for twenty years to write Johnson's life. His qualifications as the author of the inscription were seriously questioned by the appropriate committee and the final wording was a subject of much controversy. See Warren Derry, *Dr. Parr: A Portrait of the Whig Dr. Johnson* (Oxford, 1966), pp. 169–70, 176–87; *Life,* 4: 464–72.

10 See Twining's *Recreations and Studies of a Country Clergyman of the Eighteenth Century,* ed. Richard Twining (London, 1882), pp. 128–30.

11 Roger Lonsdale, *Dr. Charles Burney* (Oxford, 1965), p. 288.

12 This letter to Susan Phillips, written in December 1784, is quoted by Lonsdale, pp. 288–89. On 5 May 1785, Dr. Lort wrote Percy a letter which included the names of Cooke, Tyers, Hawkins, Kippis, and Mrs. Piozzi as future biographers of Johnson. In what now seems an ironic afterthought, Lort casually mentions Boswell's project. See Nichols, *Illustrations,* 7: 467.

13 *Gentleman's Magazine* 84 (April 1814): 420–21.

14 There were, of course, a number of satiric pieces devoted to the ridicule of biographers. But since these were primarily concerned with attacking Boswell, Piozzi, and Hawkins, they are not relevant to this discussion.

15 See, for example, Lucyle Werkmeister, *The London Daily Press, 1772–1792* (Lincoln, Neb., 1963).

16 *European Magazine* 10 (August 1786): 130.

17 Davis, p. 20. Davis's book contains a useful summary of the reception of Hawkins and other early biographers, pp. 1–36.

18 We have seen this poem in the *General Evening Post* for 18–20 May 1786, and in the *European Magazine* 9 (May 1786): 306.

19 *Critical Review* 59 (February 1785): 141–42.

20 *Town and Country Magazine* 17 (April 1785): 197.

21 *Gentleman's Magazine* 54 (December 1784): 992–93. An advertisement had appeared in the *Morning Herald* as early as 15 December. The *Life* was actually published two weeks after Johnson's death. See Chap. 3, n. 16, this volume.

22 Kearsley wrote that the *Life* was written by a "Gentleman who was long honored with the friendship of Dr. Johnson, and much better qualified, both in literary Knowledge, and Facts, than those who are daily inserting paragraphs in the Papers, evidently with no other View than to lessen the Merits of a Performance which is likely to get the Start of them in

Point of Time, Abilities, and Information." In the *Morning Herald* for 23 December Kearsley observed: "The executors of the late Dr. Johnson have no right to complain of any person, for publishing an account of the life of that justly celebrated character, especially previous to its appearance. Impartiality is, without question, more to be expected from a disinterested Editor, than from a person whose plan is influenced by lucrative views. They are alarmed lest the proposed authentic memoirs, written under the strongest impressions of candour, by a gentleman who was for many years in habits of the strictest intimacy with the Doctor, should anticipate them, and satisfy the curiosity of the public."

23 See Hazen, "*Beauties*," pp. 293–94. If Cooke did write the "Memoirs" included in the fifth edition of Kearsley's *Beauties of Johnson* (1782) as Hazen suggests, then at least a portion of the *Life* had already been written and was expanded (perhaps hastily) into a more complete biography. But see Appendix B, n. 3. The first edition was clearly printed hastily. The copy for the book, an 8 ° in 4's, was either cast off so poorly in the haste or new material was added after the printing had begun so that a four-leaf gathering 'f' and a two-leaf gathering 'g' had to be inserted between gatherings E and F. The pages of these inserted leaves are numbered 33 to 44 but are distinguished from the others of the same number by an asterisk. In addition, pages 49 and 50 (H1) contain four more lines per page.

24 See the *Critical Review* 59 (March 1785): 239–40.

The attitude of the *Monthly Review* 78 (August 1785): 147–48, was more severe. In the *English Review* 6 (September 1785): 307, the reviewer dismissed the book in three sentences as unoriginal and worthy of serving only as the frontispiece to a jest book. Since the second edition is dated 22 February 1785, Cooke had less than two months in which to revise his work. Some of the errors are corrected and there is some revision but mostly Cooke filled out the second edition by inserting blocks of materials. "Ad Urbanum," the "respectable hottentot" sketch, the epitaphs for Johnson's parents and the rules of the Essex-Head Club, for example, are simply inserted at the proper places in the narrative. He also took advantage of the Johnsoniana which appeared after the first edition in order to flesh out his characterization. See the discussion below, Chap. 3, pp. 91–108.

25 *Gentleman's Magazine* 56 (September 1786): 729–30.

26 (London, 1787), pp. 56–63. The *Dialogues* themselves received for the most part, a favorable response. The *Gentleman's Magazine* 57 (June–July 1787): 520–21, 612–14, praised them and printed excerpts. The *Scots Magazine* 49 (September 1787): 451, found their accuracy and elegance praiseworthy and their form pleasing. Arthur Murphy in the *Monthly Review* 77 (December 1787): 457–59, praised the elegance and high sprits of the *Dialogues,* but falsely accused Hayley of partiality for Chesterfield. In general, this review (which began by denouncing Johnsoniana) was

typical of those which advocated the suppression of unpleasant details in biography and lamented the dredging up of Johnson's idiosyncracies.

27 Nichols, *Illustrations,* 7: 475.

28 *English Review* 9 (February 1787): 124–26.

29 *Monthly Review* 75 (December 1786), 455–57. This review was by Ralph Griffiths.

30 *Critical Review* 62 (December 1786), 429–32.

31 A thorough search of the periodicals failed to turn up any reviews of Shaw, for example, and the only review of Tyers seems to have been that by George Steevens in an anonymous letter to the *St. James's Chronicle* for 8–11 January 1785. See Waingrow, pp. 46, 146 n. 1.

32 Due in large part to their social eminence, Mrs. Piozzi, Hawkins, and Boswell monopolized the attention of the reviewers and correspondents in the magazines and newspapers. Three studies noteworthy for their descriptions of the reception of Mrs. Piozzi, Hawkins, and Boswell are James L. Clifford, *Hester Lynch Piozzi (Mrs. Thrale),* 2nd ed. (Oxford, 1952), pp. 255–77; Davis, pp. 1–36; and Lucyle Werkmeister, *Jemmie Boswell and the London Daily Press,* pp. 1–19.

33 Joseph W. Reed, Jr., *English Biography in the Early Nineteenth Century, 1801–1838* (New Haven, 1966), p. 53.

34 Joseph Spence, *Anecdotes, Observations, and Characters, of Books and Men,* ed. James M. Osborn (Oxford, 1966), 1: xx.

Chapter Two:
JOHNSON THE WRITER

1 See Appendix A. All page references to this, and
to all the lives discussed, will be made in parenthesis
in the text. Appendix B deals with a number of the
early biographical sketches which preceded this one.

2 This survey was punctuated by two biographical
anecdotes, one of which "L" included because he
thought it was a "remarkable circumstance" (p. 92).
Unfortunately, the anecdote dealing with Edward
Cave's alleged cheating of Johnson on the proceeds
of *London,* was false, as shown by James L. Clifford,
Young Sam Johnson (New York, 1955), p. 190. Clifford, however, cites the inaccuracy of this story in
Shaw, not in "L."

3 The observations on *Irene* and the comparison of
Johnson's prose to poetry were largely taken from the
Companion to the Play-House. See Appendix B. This
remark about Johnson's prose seems to have begun
with David Erskine Baker's interpretation of William
Rider's "About three Years ago he published *Rassilas*
[sic], *Prince of Abyssinia,* a Novel in the oriental Way,
a Species of Writing, which is near of Kin to Poetry,
and in which Mr. *Johnson* is allowed to surpass all
English Authors." See Appendix A. The observation
that Johnson's prose was like poetry quickly became a
critical commonplace. Anna Seward in a letter to Boswell, 25 March 1785, went so far as to claim that
"Every thing Johnson wrote was poetry; for the poetic

essence consists not in rhyme and measure, which are only its trappings, but in the strength, and glow of the fancy, to which all the works of art and nature stand in prompt administration . . . ." Waingrow, p. 80.

4 For a survey of contemporary opinion on the *Dictionary*, see Gertrude E. Noyes, "The Critical Reception of Johnson's *Dictionary* in the Latter Eighteenth Century," *Modern Philology* 52 (February 1955): 175–91.

5 See the *Companion to the Play-House*, Appendix B.

6 The identification of much of Johnson's writings was left to Boswell. See *Life*, 1: 16–24. Boswell did his best to ascertain the authenticity of Johnson's works from Johnson himself, from internal evidence, and from previous ascriptions. See R. W. Chapman, *Two Centuries of Johnsonian Scholarship* (Glasgow, 1945), pp. 8–12, 18–20; and Greene, pp. 407–27. Greene maintains that Boswell's authority is no more trustworthy than that of Tyers, Hawkins, or Tom Davies (p. 420).

7 Greene, p. 408. See also Johnson's letter to William Strahan of 20 January 1759, where he says that he would not set his name to *Rasselas* because he expected his authorship to be known. *Letters*, 1: 118.

8 Greene, p. 415.

9 See Appendix A. It is possible that Isaac Reed wrote this account. It is known that Reed wrote biographical and critical essays for the *European Magazine* (see Appendix B, n. 2) and that he had an "extensive and accurate knowledge of English literary History" (*Life*,

4: 37) which Johnson had drawn upon for his *Lives of the Poets*. Since most of Johnson's works were published anonymously, the author of this account must have known Johnson and have had enough interest in literary history to feel compelled to collect this information. Boswell certainly felt that Reed would have information about Johnson's publications at his fingertips when he asked him to send "a chronological note of what you understand to be written by Johnson between 1757 and 1765 inclusive. My servant will call tomorrow before 12 for your answer" (*Letters of James Boswell*, 2: 396). George Steevens is also a very likely candidate. See Davis, p. 47. Dr. Richard Brocklesby in a letter to Boswell, 13 December 1784, reports hearing that Steevens had taken away the Catalog of Johnson's works. This Catalog served, no doubt, as the basis of the *Account*. Waingrow suggests that it was probably written by Steevens, though he may have had some help from Reed. See Waingrow, pp. 26, 146 n. 1.

10 See "Boswell's Predecessors and Editors," *A Paladin of Philanthropy* (London, 1899), p. 140, for Dobson's comment; for Greene's, pp. 409, 417.

11 He was the only biographer to reprint Smollett's letter, or even to recount the anecdote. The story was merely inserted in the midst of the list of Johnson's productions with no attempt to establish its context.

12 Greene, p. 415, accepts this testimony. Because he overlooks "L's" account, Greene's praise of the *Account* is slightly exaggerated.

13 Greene, p. 415; the preface to Raleigh's work is an attribution that still requires scrutiny.

14 Ibid.

15 Boswell denied Johnson's authorship of these pieces on the basis of internal evidence. *Life,* 1: 19.

16 See Appendix A. We have been unable to locate an advertisement giving the exact date of publication, but since Shaw refers to the "late" Tom Davies it must have appeared after 5 May 1785.

17 As James L. Clifford shows in his essay, "Some Problems of Johnson's Obscure Middle Years," *Johnson, Boswell and Their Circle: Essays Presented to Lawrence Fitzroy Powell* (Oxford, 1965), pp. 99–110, gaps in information still abound even for the years when Johnson was famous.

18 Chapman reprints them in his edition of the *Letters,* 1: 30, 34, 39–40; 2: 253.

19 See Greene, p. 416.

20 Shaw also accused Johnson of a "warped" mind in his treatment of Swift.

21 Shaw's linking of Johnson's poetry with Pope's may seem especially odd, since the music of their verses could scarcely be more different. But as early as 1764 the *Companion* sketch had stated that "in Verse his Numbers are harmonious and musical, yet bold and poignant, and on the whole approach nearer to Mr. Pope's Manner of Versification than that of any other Writer . . . ." See Appendix B.

22 See Donald J. Greene, *The Politics of Samuel Johnson* (New Haven, 1960), pp. 121–22.

23 See *Life,* 3: 106, 488, where Boswell reprinted Shaw's expression of gratitude for Johnson's help in this undertaking.

24 *Life,* 3: 488. In a letter to Johnson dated 4 April 1777, Boswell reported that he had read Shaw's "Proposal" for the *Galic and English Dictionary,* noting that they were "written *by the hand of a* MASTER." *Letters of James Boswell,* 1: 260.

25 See *Letters,* 2: 408. In a letter to Boswell of 11 March 1777, Johnson called Shaw a "modest and decent man," *Letters,* 2: 164–65.

26 Shaw carefully explained, for example, Johnson's initial reaction to his theory that the Ossian poems were impostures (pp. 154–56).

27 See *Life,* 4: 526, for a list of the pamphlets exchanged during this debate. For an account of the response in the newspapers and magazines, see Helen Louise McGuffie's unpublished dissertation, "Samuel Johnson and the Hostile Press" (Columbia, 1961).

28 See Appendix A. The *General Evening Post* for 10 October 1786 announced that the *Essay* would be published the next Thursday, and on Thursday, 12 October the book was announced as published. As late as 8 December 1786 the *Morning Chronicle* carried an announcement of its publication.

29 *DNB* and Raleigh, *Six Essays on Johnson* (Oxford, 1910), p. 42.

30 See Chap. 2, p. 25.

31 By Greene, *The Politics of Samuel Johnson,* pp. 231–58.

32 *Lives,* 3: 361–62.

33 In 1775, Towers had written *A Letter to Dr. Samuel Johnson, occasioned by his late political Publications.* See *Life,* 2: 316. Boswell reprinted excerpts from the *Letter* and concluded: "I am willing to do justice to the merit of Dr. Towers, of whom I will say, that although I abhor his Whiggish democratical notions and propensities . . . I esteem him as an ingenious, knowing, and very convivial man."

34 *Life,* 4: 41, n. 1.

Chapter Three:
JOHNSON THE MORALIST

1 Hobhouse's poem, a rare work, can be found in *The Works of the British Poets,* ed. Thomas Parks (London, 1808), 13: 5–7. Other noteworthy epitaphs and elegies were written by Anna Seward, William Woty, and William Cowper. Maurice Quinlan, "The Rumor of Dr. Johnson's Conversion," *Review of Religion* 12 (March 1948), 243–45, discusses the implications of Cowper's epitaph regarding Johnson's supposed conversion to Christianity on his death bed. Many of the poetic remembrances of Johnson can be found in a scrapbook of clippings from eighteenth-century newspapers compiled by Lieutenant-Colonel Francis Richard Charles Grant, author of the *Life of Samuel Johnson* (London, 1887), loaned to us by Mr. Herman W. Liebert.

2   The epithet is Austin Dobson's. See "Boswell's Predecessors and Editors," p. 141.

3   It was Johnson himself who introduced Tyers to Boswell. See *Life*, 2: 107. Tyers said that he met Johnson through Christopher Smart, and that he had known Johnson for thirty years.

4   *Life*, 3: 308. Boswell used to call Tyers "Tiresias" as a pun on his name. Ibid.: 523.

5   Ibid.: 308. According to the article on Tyers in the *DNB* written by Warwick William Wroth, Tyers was supposed to have described himself in a sketch as "inquisitive, talkative, full of notions and quotations, and, which is the praise of a purling stream, of no great depth.' "

6   *Life*, 3: 308, n. 3; Nichols, *Anecdotes*, 8: 81; Gerald Dennis Meyer, Introduction to Tyers's *Sketch*, Augustan Reprint Society, no. 34 (Los Angeles, 1952), p. iii.

7   *Life*, 3: 309. Johnson once admitted that Tyers always told him something he had not known before. See Nichols, *Anecdotes*, 8: 88.

8   See Appendix A. Robina Napier, *Johnsoniana* (London, 1884), pp. 171–93, and G. B. Hill, *Johnsonian Miscellanies*, 2: 335–81, reprinted Tyers's *Sketch*, but used the version which appeared in the *Gentleman's Magazine*, not the pamphlet which corrected some errors and was nearly a third longer. Because Hill used the earlier version, he implied that Tyers was careless. The pamphlet version is extremely rare. According to the account in the *DNB*, Tyers issued only fifty copies of his essay on Addison in the first

edition and one hundred in the second. His short biography of Pope was issued in only 250 copies. Meyer says that Tyers printed only a few copies of the *Sketch* for his friends (p. i).

9   *Life,* 3: 309.

10   See Meyer, pp. iv–v, and *Life,* 3: 308–09.

11   In 1788, of course, Mrs. Piozzi published her correspondence with Johnson.

12   Meyer, pp. ii–iii, lists the anecdotes which Tyers reported for the first time.

13   See *Life,* 3: 307, and n. 2. Boswell originally recorded Tyers's remark in the *Journal of a Tour to the Hebrides,* ed. Frederick A. Pottle and Charles H. Bennett (New York, 1936, 1962), p. 50; *Life,* 5:73.

14   To heighten further the effect of Johnson's conversation, Tyers contrasted Johnson's unbecoming appearance with his moral and intellectual power, but gave this contrast a twist by asserting that Johnson's very shabbiness led to the expectation of underlying greatness (p. 17).

15   Greene, pp. 415, 416.

16   See Appendix A; and Chap. 1, pp. 11–13. The title page is dated 1785 but the book is dated 28 December. Advertisements in the *Morning Herald* and the *St. James's Chronicle* indicated that it was to be published on Monday, 27 December 1784. See Davis, pp. v, 3. The second edition is dated 22 February 1785. Excerpts from Cooke were included in *Johnsonian Miscellanies,* 2: 161–70.

17   Donald A. Stauffer, *The Art of Biography in*

Eighteenth Century England (Princeton, 1941), 2: 313–14.

18   Hazen, "*Beauties*," 294–95; and Appendix B, n. 3.

19   Greene, p. 416. Cooke also made other attributions in *The Beauties of Johnson* (see Greene, p. 414).

20   Page numbers refer to the second edition of 1785 unless otherwise indicated.

21   See Chap. 1, n. 23.

22   Boswell appreciated Cooke's portrait of Johnson's odd manner of walking, calling it "just and picturesque." *Life,* 4: 71.

23   In the first edition (pp. 13–14) Cooke weighed the evidence rather carefully before concluding that Johnson's marriage was a love match rather than one of convenience. In the second edition this section is revised and the question of the marriage being one of convenience is not mentioned. Perhaps Cooke felt that the statements in the first edition compromised Johnson as moral hero. The confusion was compounded when in the first edition he erroneously assigned *Idler* No. 41 to the memory of Johnson's wife when actually it was written in memory of his mother who had died shortly before. He corrected this mistake for the second edition.

24   In the first edition he went so far as to state that "learning and literary men formed almost the whole of Johnson's business and amusement" (p. 91).

25   This statement echoes that in the *Companion to the Play-House*. See Appendix B.

26   See *Johnsonian Miscellanies,* 1: 466.

27   His statements concerning the *Idler* in the second edition were much more temperate than those in the first. In the first edition he argued that *"humour* was not the Doctor's *strong hold"* because it was "rather *dry* and *pointed,* than *easy* and *natural"*; therefore, he contended, the *Idler,* less serious than the *Rambler,* was a second-rate performance (pp. 35–36). Humor, of course, need not vitiate morality. And there need be no incompatibility between the two kinds of humor discussed by Cooke, but Johnson certainly was skilled in both, although the dryness was more pronounced in his writings and light humor in his conversation. It is certain that Cooke failed to see Johnson's humor and, in any case, much preferred the "heavier" writings.

28   Italics added. Pages 115–54 of the second edition were devoted to "Johnsoniana: or Bon-Mots, Observations, &c. of the Late Dr. Samuel Johnson."

29   See Appendix A. On 13 October 1785 the *St. James's Chronicle* announced that the first number of the *Dictionary* printed by J. Jarvis and sold by J. Fielding would be available on Saturday, 15 October. "Fielding's Genuine Edition of Dr. Johnson's Dictionary" was to appear in 48 quarto numbers complete with a Bartolozzi print. On 30 November the *General Evening Post* carried an advertisement maintaining the superiority of this edition over its rivals and announcing that "The Life of Dr. Johnson, written by a gentleman of the first literary abilities, will be given at the conclusion of the Dictionary." If one number ap-

peared a week, as planned, the life must have been available about September 1786. The author of this life has not, to our knowledge, been identified. This life should not be confused with the brief life, supposedly by James Harrison, prefixed to the Harrison edition of the *Dictionary* (1786). This life which fills eighteen unnumbered pages at the beginning of the volume is little more than an abridgement of Hawkins's *Life* with an occasional look at Mrs. Piozzi's *Anecdotes* and several other of the early lives. The *London Chronicle* announced on 17 October 1785 that the dictionary would be printed in 100 6d numbers beginning 22 October. (The first number is not advertised as published, however, until 8 November.) On 21 March 1786 it was announced that a portrait would be ready tomorrow for those with notes given with the first twenty numbers. It is almost impossible at this date to figure out just how the work was distributed in 100 numbers. If the numbers were given out on schedule, the dictionary would have been completed about September 1787, but since the life is printed on unsigned folio gatherings it is impossible to tell when it might have been supplied to the subscriber. Because of its indebtedness to Hawkins, it is likely that it appeared between March and September 1787. It is, in fact, very probable that the life appeared before September in order to ride the crest of Hawkins's popularity. See Davis, pp. 14ff.

30   Equally narrow was his comment on Johnson's

parliamentary reporting which, he said, featured "mischievous elegance that destroys the discrimination of character, and subverts the reality of History" (p. 8).

Chapter Four:
"NO SPECIES OF WRITING SEEMS MORE WORTHY
OF CULTIVATION THAN BIOGRAPHY"

1 Although it is known, for example, that Boswell used a number of anecdotes from Tyers and took the text of the 1739 Lord Gower letter from Cooke, it is often difficult to establish with any degree of certainty whether he gleaned a given piece of information from the early lives or whether he arrived at the information independently. In several instances he and one or another of his rivals had a common source of information. Both Boswell and Shaw found Mrs. Desmoulins useful and Dr. Richard Brocklesby seems to have supplied information not only to Boswell, but to Hawkins and Cooke as well. No doubt Boswell found some useful information in these early lives but, more important, his biographical predecessors served as standards by which his own performance could be judged. See Davis, pp. 103–05, 178–79; and Waingrow, pp. 25–28, 48 n. 3, 160 n. 9.
2 Ernest Jones, *The Life and Work of Sigmund Freud,* ed. and abridged by Steven Marcus and Lionel Trilling (New York, 1961), p. viii.

1 Appendix A is a list of these early lives.

2 Hazen, *"Beauties,"* p. 293, suggests that this sketch is probably by Isaac Reed (1742–1807) but gives no support for his attribution. John Nichols in his "Biographical Memoir of the late Isaac Reed, Esq." [*Gentleman's Magazine* 77 (January 1807): 80] states that Reed was "a valuable contributor to the Westminster Magazine from 1773–4 to about the year 1780. The biographical articles are from his pen." The quotation continues: "He became also very early one of the proprietors of the *European Magazine,* and was a constant contributor to it for many years, particularly in the biographical and critical departments." This would certainly leave open the possibility that the "Account" in the *European Magazine* was written by Reed. See Chap. 2, n. 9. This information concerning Reed's connections with the *Westminster* and *European* magazines was repeated the next month by James Bindley in his "An Account of Isaac Reed, Esq.," *European Magazine* 51: 83; and later repeated in Nichols, *Anecdotes,* 2: 667; and in the account in the *DNB.*

3 Since Cooke incorporated two-thirds of the "Memoir" into his *Life,* he too is indebted to the *Biographia Dramatica.* See Hazen, *"Beauties,"* p. 293. One of the arguments put forward by Hazen for Cooke's authorship of the "Memoirs" is the unlikelihood "that a second author would ever adopt so wholeheartedly, with no attempt at concealment, variety or revision, the work of his predecessor." It should be clear from this study that the early biographers of Johnson, at least, had no such scruples. The fifth edition of the *Beauties* was announced as published 22 April 1782 in the *St. James's Chronicle*. (The "Advertisement" to the edition is dated 16 April 1782.) We have not been able to locate an advertisement announcing the publication of the *Biographia Dramatica*, but it was available by the end of January 1782, for a quotation from the sketch on Johnson is given in the *St. James's Chronicle* for 30 January. Reviews appeared in both the *European* and *Gentleman's* magazines for February 1782. Since the *Gentleman's Magazine* quotes the entire Johnson sketch, the author of the "Memoir" may have used it.

4   This letter was reprinted in Cooke's *Life*, the *European Magazine* "Account," Shaw's *Memoirs*, Hawkins and Boswell. See Davis, pp. 103–05. A variant version of this letter had appeared earlier in Sir Herbert Croft's *Love and Madness* (pp. 71–72) which was announced as published in the *St. James Chronicle*, 14–16 March 1780. Croft states that the letter was shown him by a clergyman who assured him that it was authentic (p. 70). Both this volume and the *Beauties* were published by G. Kearsley.

5   The 1764 edition read: ". . . received his Education and took his Degrees at the University of *Oxford,* after quitting which Place I have been informed he for some Time was Master of a private Academy at

Litchfield. — A Genius like his, however, could not long content itself with that most disagreeable of all Drudgery, the mere classical Instruction of Youth, nor suffer its Brightness to be conceal'd in the dull Obscurity of a Country Academy. — He came up therefore to *London,* where he immediately gave Proofs how high a Rank in the World of Letters he deserved to hold."